Top Notes

Selected Poems:
Rosemary Dobson

Study notes for Common Module:
Texts and Human Experiences
2019–2023 HSC

Suzan Pattinson

A
FIVE SENSES
PUBLICATION

Five Senses Education Pty Ltd
2/195 Prospect Highway
Seven Hills 2147
New South Wales
Australia

Pattinson, Suzan
Top Notes – Rosemary Dobson
ISBN 978-1-76032-245-8

CONTENTS

TOP NOTES SERIES

This series has been created to assist HSC students of English in their understanding of set texts. Top Notes are easy to read, providing analysis of issues and discussion of important ideas contained in the texts.

Particular care has been taken to ensure that students are able to examine each text in the context of the module it has been allocated to.

Each text generally includes:

- Notes on the specific module
- Plot summary
- Character analysis
- Setting
- Thematic concerns
- Language studies
- Essay questions and a modelled response
- Other textual material
- Study practice questions
- Useful quotes

We have covered the areas we feel are important for students in their study of *Texts and Human Experiences* for their Common Module. I am sure you will find these Top Notes useful in your studies of English.

Bruce Pattinson
Series Editor

COMMON MODULE:
TEXTS AND HUMAN EXPERIENCES

*"It is quite possible—overwhelmingly probable, one might guess—
that we will always learn more about human life and personality
from novels than from scientific psychology"*

NOAM CHOMSKY

What is the Common Module?

The Common Module set for the 2019–23 HSC is *Texts and Human
Experiences*. It is compulsory to study this topic as prescribed by
NESA and it is common to all three English courses. Remember:
you will be learning how texts reveal individual and collective
human experiences. There are no right or wrong answers in this
module – it is about how you see and interpret material and
engage with it.

In the Common Module you will be analysing one prescribed text
and a range of short texts that are related to the idea of human
experiences. You will analyse texts not only to investigate the
ideas they present about this area but also how they convey these
ideas. This means you will be looking closely at the techniques a
composer uses to represent his / her messages and shape meaning.
You will also be looking at relationships between texts in regard
to the experiences you explore. Overall, you will become an
expert on texts and the human experience — that is, the different
notions people have about human experience and the various
ways composers manipulate techniques to communicate their
ideas about it.

Specifically you will look at one set text from the following list.

- Doerr, Anthony, *All the Light We Cannot See*
- Lohrey, Amanda, *Vertigo*
- Orwell, George, *Nineteen Eighty-Four*
- Parrett, Favel, *Past the Shallows*
- Dobson, Rosemary 'Young Girl at a Window', 'Over the Hill', 'Summer's End', 'The Conversation', 'Cock Crow', 'Amy Caroline', 'Canberra Morning'
- Slessor, Kenneth 'Wild Grapes', 'Gulliver', 'Out of Time', 'Vesper-Song of the Reverend Samuel Marsden', 'William Street', 'Beach Burial'
- Harrison, Jane, *Rainbow's End*
- Miller, Arthur, *The Crucible*
- Shakespeare, William, *The Merchant of Venice*
- Winton, Tim, *The Boy Behind the Curtain* Chapters: 'Havoc: A Life in Accidents', 'Betsy', 'Twice on Sundays', 'The Wait and the Flow', 'In the Shadow of the Hospital', 'The Demon Shark', 'Barefoot in the Temple of Art'
- Yousafzai, Malala & Lamb, Christina, *I am Malala*
- Daldry, Stephen, *Billy Elliot*
- O'Mahoney, Ivan, *Go Back to Where You Came From* – Series 1, Episodes 1, 2 and 3 and *The Response*
- Walker, Lucy, *Waste Land*

NESA has mandated that students must study a related text as part of the common module, and that this should be part of their in-school assessment. However there is NO LONGER a requirement to write about a related text in the HSC examination itself.

WHAT DOES NESA REQUIRE FOR THE COMMON MODULE?

The NESA documentation of the Common Module: Texts and Human Experiences states that students:

- deepen their understanding of how texts represent individual and collective human experiences;

- examine how texts represent human qualities and emotions associated with, or arising from, these experiences;

- appreciate, explore, interpret, analyse and evaluate the ways language is used to shape these representations in a range of texts in a variety of forms, modes and media;

- explore how texts may give insight into the anomalies, paradoxes and inconsistencies in human behaviour and motivations, inviting the responder to see the world differently, to challenge assumptions, ignite new ideas or reflect personally;

- may also consider the role of storytelling throughout time to express and reflect particular lives and cultures;

- by responding to a range of texts, further develop skills and confidence using various literary devices, language concepts, modes and media to formulate a considered response to texts;

- study one prescribed text and a range of short texts that provide rich opportunities to further explore representations of human experiences illuminated in texts;

- make increasingly informed judgements about how aspects of these texts, for example, context, purpose, structure, stylistic and grammatical features, and form shape meaning;

- select one related text and draw from personal experience to make connections between themselves, the world of the text and their wider world;

- by responding and composing throughout the module, further develop a repertoire of skills in comprehending, interpreting and analysing complex texts;

- examine how different modes and media use visual, verbal and/or digital language elements;

- communicate ideas using figurative language to express universal themes and evaluative language to make informed judgements about texts;

- further develop skills in using metalanguage, correct grammar and syntax to analyse language and express a personal perspective about a text

If this is what is required by NESA, we need to examine the concept of human experience carefully so we can adequately respond in these ways. I would recommend that you read the complete document which is on the NESA web site and can be downloaded in Word or Adobe. Understanding this document is an important step in handling the textual material within the guidelines required—remember you are reading for a purpose and should make notes and highlight ideas as you read so that you can develop these ideas later.

UNDERSTANDING THE COMMON MODULE

What are Human Experiences?

The concept of Human Experiences is at the heart of the Common Module.

Human Experiences are experiences of individuals or a group of people (eg a family, society, or nation) in life. There are a very wide range of human experiences which include but go beyond this list:

- feelings or reactions (momentary or long term): love, hate, anger, joy, fear, disgust
- key milestones or stages: birth, childhood, adulthood, marriage, divorce, death
- culture, belonging and identity
- conformity and rebellion
- innocence and guilt, justice
- freedom and repression
- education, vocation, work, sport, leisure
- attraction to a person, idea, group or cause
- opposition to an idea, cause, political system
- religious faith or belief
- extreme events such as an earthquake, avalanche, tsuanami
- regular events such as walking, eating, singing, dancing, discussing ideas.

The word *experience* seems innately connected to the human condition and it is something we have each day whether a mundane experience that is repetitive, or something new and dramatic which offers challenges and rewards. Experiences can vary greatly in their impact on individuals, groups and countries. One example might be a war that is a negative experience for a whole population while we may experience the wonder of medicine with a new vaccine for a deadly disease that saves millions of people. We need to note that the module asks for 'experiences' ...we are a combination of different experiences and each has a varying impact. One person's problem is another's challenge depending on perspective, skill set, previous experience and ability.

Experiences are widespread and often shared: this is why people tell their stories and these shared experiences form part of our cultural heritage. These experiences often inform, warn and teach across entire cultural groups and many stories are shared across cultures.

DEFINING HUMAN EXPERIENCES

Now let's attempt to define what human experiences are and shape them into a more coherent and easily understood framework so we can begin our investigation at a basic level of understanding before moving into more complex analysis and looking at how the texts illuminate our understanding of the term.

Dictionary.com defines the term **experience** as:

noun

1. a particular instance of personally encountering or undergoing something:

2. the process or fact of personally observing, encountering, or undergoing something:

3. the observing, encountering, or undergoing of things generally as they occur in the course of time:
   to learn from experience; the range of human experience.

4. knowledge or practical wisdom gained from what one has observed, encountered, or undergone, e.g. *a man of experience.*

5. *Philosophy.* the totality of the cognitions given by perception; all that is perceived, understood, and remembered.

verb

(used with object), **experienced, experiencing.**

6. to have experience of; meet with; undergo; feel, e.g. *to experience nausea.*

7. to learn by experience.

idiom

8. **experience religion**, to undergo a spiritual conversion by which one gains or regains faith in God.

Obviously there are a number of definitions according to context, but all are applicable to our study in some shape or form, as the range of human experience is so vast. The search for 'new experience' has driven much of the development of people, groups, cultures and nations over past millennia. New experiences are always met with excitement and often trepidation as to what change they might bring.

Think historically about how people have reacted to change. It can cause great upheavals in society, with violent reactions while other changes brought through various experiences are welcomed and may change how people live and comprehend the world. Experiences affect us emotionally in many cases rather than logically and when we respond emotionally, behaviours become unpredictable. This causes the paradoxes, anomalies and inconsistencies mentioned in the rubric. If we were logical beings the world would be an easier place, but probably more boring.

These definitions all point to the fact that memory is the key to experience. The experience is stored in memory and drawn upon when the circumstances are repeated or closely mimicked so we can deal with them — hopefully better than on the initial experience.

Experiences can come in many ways and the synonyms listed below for experience help us to understand the concept even further. They assist in defining how an experience can arise:

Synonyms

actions	understanding	judgment
background	wisdom	observation
contacts	acquaintances	perspicacity
involvement	actuality	practicality
know-how	caution	proofs
maturity	combat	savoir-faire
participation	doings	seasonings
patience	empiricism	sophistication
practice	evidence	strife
reality	existences	trials
sense	exposures	worldliness
skill	familiarity	forebearance
struggle	intimacy	
training	inwardness	

http://www.thesaurus.com/browse/experience?s=t

These synonyms show partly the vast array of words that our language has created around this concept, and also shows how important it is in the human psyche. We, as humans, want to experience. Now we will look at some examples of experiences and examine how they can have an impact. It is also important to remember that experiences do not have to be positive. You might experience a huge problem, a bereavement, a car accident, an unwelcome relationship or something totally bizarre that rocks your world. There can be a more opaque side to any experience that may need to be addressed.

The whole aim of this Common Module is to examine the text closely but also relate it to the concept of human experiences and decide how examining it in this way enables us to better understand both the text and the concept of humanity.

It is important that you unpack what each text you study shows you about human experiences and what ideas / themes arise from those experiences. Formulate your own ideas about the text.

Read the NESA Stage 6 document called *English Stage 6: Annotations of selected texts prescribed for the Higher School Certificate 2019-23* (see *www.educationstandards.nsw.edu.au*) for the set text you are studying. This document offers insights into the way each particular text should be examined by outlining key ideas and areas for clarification.

Human experiences and ways of experiencing vary due to individual circumstance and these experiences can change many things about individual lives, communities and the world. When we examine the concept of human experience in relation to a text, we need to examine the assumptions or biases we bring to it as well as how experiencing the text itself may change us and how we view things. The text may challenge and confront how we view the human experience or we may have preconceived ideas that make it more difficult for this to happen.

Students can also think about their own 'personal experience to make connections between themselves, the world of the text and their wider world.' Examining and enjoying any text is an experience in itself but it is what we take away from the text and apply that is the crucial aspect. That is not to say that every text will be enjoyed or offer a human experience that is significant either positively or negatively. Some texts may not personally engage you and that is fine. This is especially so when you begin to look for other related material that links to *Texts and Human Experiences*. We recommend that you find examples of texts that link but also personally appeal to you so that you can relate empathetically with them.

Individual Human Experiences

The idea of personal experiences is a popular and pervasive concept, especially in the literature of many cultures. Recording personal experiences as a means of sharing wisdom or more mundane daily tasks is part of human nature and we record and relate these experiences frequently. Experiences are recorded and relayed in many ways. We tell oral stories in both anecdotal and formal ways, we write, draw, sing and photograph our way into history (or not). Look at the proliferation of social media in this current century as people record their daily, even hourly, experiences for all to see. We record the most trivial details of our lives for likes and followers while the real world passes us by. Human experiences affect us on a daily basis and some experiences influence our lives and the way we live them.

Individuals seek out experiences in a variety of ways. Some seek more and more extreme experiences to test themselves against the world. Others limit their experiences. A lot of people prefer the familiar and don't actively seek new experiences. Individuals, it must be remembered, also see experiences in different ways and the same experience may have a very different impact on individuals. The one thing we can be certain about is that experiences are part of humanity and even the most limited of us have them. Many of these experiences also come from interaction with others and as noted we also like to share these experiences.

Experiences are what define us in many ways and are what makes us human.

We are going to look at four specific ways that experiences can influence us as people over the next few pages. These are physical, psychological, emotional and intellectual experiences and many experiences are a combination of these.

Physical Experience

The concept of a physical experience is tied into the human experience and part of the collective experience as well. Individuals seek physical experiences to test themselves against nature and other individuals often as part of trials and rituals, for example being integrated into a community. In modern times individuals have sought to test themselves with extreme sports and explorations into the harshest conditions and even space. Physical experiences can also change the way we see the world and others because of the chemical changes these experiences have on our bodies and mind. Physical experiences are often challenges and part of the experience is overcoming adversity. These physical challenges are often celebrated, as in the case of sports, but can also offer challenges if the experience is a negative one such as an accident or disease. Physical experiences are also often quite public and thus have permeated our societies in both their execution and how they are perceived. These physical experiences, even if experienced vicariously, have become popular across cultures and celebrated. Think of examples for yourself but most competitive sports offer examples.

Bruce Lee extends the concept of the physical experience into all aspects of life and that's what we will look at next in our analysis of human experiences –

'If you always put limits on everything you do, physical or anything else, it will spread into your work and into your life. There are no limits. There are only plateaus, and you must not stay there, you must go beyond them.'

Psychological Experience

The idea of a psychological experience is tied into many of the abstract ideas that people experience and can lead to a discussion of what is normal psychology. From the earliest times humans have attempted to alter their psychology through a number of experiences. On a simple level this can be a drug that changes the person's or group's perspective on reality. Examples of this might be alcohol or marijuana but cultural groups also use various substances to share group experiences. This can be seen in Native American cultures with *peyote*. In more modern times prescription drugs that are mood altering have been used to minimise the symptoms of psychiatric illnesses such as depression, and these mood altering drugs are common and legal. Others attempt to alter their psychology by seeing specialists in this area while others act out their condition leading to social and criminal issues. When discussing the human experience, psychology is a key issue and will form a part of most studies of experience. When taken too far this search for a new psychological experience can be harmful eg. an addiction.

Carl Jung, the famous psychologist, comments on the problems of addiction for human experiences, stating clearly that excess can be an issue:

"Every form of addiction is bad, no matter whether the narcotic be alcohol, morphine or idealism."

Emotional Experience

According to the psychologist, Robert Plutchik, there are eight basic emotions:

- **Fear** — feeling afraid.
- **Anger** — feeling angry. A stronger word for anger is rage.
- **Sadness** — feeling sad. Other words are sorrow, grief (a stronger feeling, for example when someone has died) or **depression** (feeling sad for a long time without any external cause). Some people think depression is a different emotion.
- **Joy** — feeling happy. Other words are happiness, gladness.
- **Disgust** — feeling something is wrong or nasty
- **Trust** — a positive emotion; admiration is stronger; **acceptance** is weaker
- **Anticipation** — in the sense of looking forward positively to something which is going to happen. **Expectation** is more neutral; **dread** is more negative.

https://simple.wikipedia.org/wiki/List_of_emotions

Emotions are the strongest drivers of human experience and form lasting aspects of any experience. Think about breaking up with someone you love and the emotions that drive behaviours in this situation. People have all sorts of extreme behaviours under the influence of emotions and these experiences are often the ones recorded and those which influence us most. Think about the role emotions play in our lives and the range of emotions from the list above. Consider how much emotions affect our life experiences, how they influence our decisions which decide our experiences and on a higher level consider how they affect the decisions which may seriously impact our experiences, such as politicians going to war.

Intellectual Experience

The concept of an intellectual experience is linked to decisions and experiences we have based on analysis and logic rather than the emotional choices referred to in the previous section. These intellectual experiences have changed the way we live and how we have seen our world. These experiences have affected the way we as humans have altered our world to suit our needs and lead to all the great advances in human society and thus experiences. Changes in our ideas, beliefs etc. alter the way we interact with the world and often these intellectual changes come at great cost.

Think of the time in Europe when the Church dominated and stopped scientific advances by calling them heresy/witchcraft. Open societies are more open to new ideas and this is what has hastened the pace of intellectual experiences as dominant ideologies fall away. Intellectual advances may not have the excitement that the other types produce but perhaps they have a more lasting impact on people, societies and the world in general. Ideas are powerful experiences and people hold beliefs strongly.

Immanuel Kant stated that:

> *"experience without theory is blind, but theory without experience is mere intellectual play."*

Consider this statement in the light of what we have learnt about human experiences. Are they a combination of many factors or can we isolate experiences into simple forms?

What exactly is a human experience?

The titular question reminds us of the old brainteaser: "If a tree falls in a forest and no one is around to hear it, does it make a sound?"

There are two classic responses to this. The more Platonically-minded would say the tree always makes a sound when it falls in the forest. We don't have to be there to hear it; we can imagine the sound of a tree falling in the forest, based on memory of such an event or on the recording of such an event. We know that sound is just vibrating air, and it's safe to say that air always vibrates in response to a tree falling, or a bear growling, or a cicada singing, whether we are there to hear it or not.

The second answer is a more post-structuralist response: the sound doesn't occur on its own; it needs a human ear to be heard. Therefore, if there is no human in the forest to hear the tree fall, then there is no sound. This automatically implies that "experience" of anything requires the presence of a human being, which means there is no such thing as an experience that *isn't* human.

Animal rights activists – or anyone with a beloved pet – would almost certainly reject this notion because it prioritises humans and relegates all other species to a lower class of being: an attitude that most would agree has gotten the human race into an awful lot of environmental trouble over the last 200 years of industrialisation.

In his article (*What is an Experience?*), my learned colleague Paul Hartley describes experience in its most basic form, as "the perception of something else" and "ultimately information about what we have perceived." But does this make it particularly human? Dogs and cats perceive things. Insects perceive things. You could even say that plants perceive things, such as the direction from which the sun is shining. Perception is the most basic of life's survival tools for all manner of flora and fauna.

In her brief but cogent disquisition on the subject (*What is Human?*), another of my learned colleagues, Nadine Hare, asserts that to be human is a social construct. Hartley builds on that notion by suggesting that culture affects experience when we start to share it, because "the words, associations, and priorities we attach to the shared experience define how we understand the world we live in."

Hare rightly points out that this world is increasingly dominated by consumerism, which has distorted what it means to be human by excluding all of the attributes and qualities that "make people people." Calling us consumers reduces our experiences to mere transactions. It defines human experience within the narrow confines of the purchase funnel and has little interest in anything that isn't a purchase driver.

Perhaps the field of commerce is where the experiential rubber most emphatically meets the road. Unlike mere perception, commerce is a uniquely human experience. It has mediated, automated, and dominated the human agenda to the point where we are defined by what we buy and little else. Commerce has invaded the non-profit spheres of government, health, and education, imposing its own priorities and principles on these institutions in the expectation that they will behave more like businesses. And even though business still strives to appeal to the so-called masses, it prioritises the pursuit of individual wealth, and in so doing, not only inhibits the desire for shared experience but unravels the social fabric historically woven by the democratic tradition.

As if in response, that social fabric is being re-woven by our networks. As Hare asserts, "humans both produce technology and are produced through technology." Experience is shared more now than it ever has been because the experiential platform – i.e., that very human invention called the internet – is in place to facilitate it like never before, and on a global scale.

This sharing capability reintroduces all of those things that "make people people" back into the conversation – whether commercial or political. What "makes people people" is messy, unpredictable, emotional, and complex. Most of what makes us human has no place in the experiential confines of the purchase funnel, and defies any of our attempts to place it there.

The challenge for us as a species is to embrace this new capacity for sharing to keep the agendas of our hegemonic institutions – whether commercial or political – from defining what makes an experience human. A post-consumer business strategy might be one that, as Hare hopes, will "expand our view of people to include the complex and dynamic social, cultural, gendered, spiritual and racialised beings that they are." Maybe then will our shared human experience truly become, as Hartley asserts, the glue that holds us all together as human beings.

Will Novosedlik
MISC magazine

https://miscmagazine.com/what-is-a-human-experience/

This article appeared in the September 2014 edition of MISC magazine. Can you relate to what the article says about human experiences? Do human experiences depend on perception? Does the experience of anything require the presence of a human as experiencer (para 3)? Can the ideas of experience be extended to include perception by plants or animals? Hartley's idea is that "shared human experience" is "the glue that holds us all together as human beings". Is this an oversimplification?

The Impact of Human Experiences

Human experiences have impacts on many levels. On an individual level, we can have changes in our assumptions about the world and people around us; we can ingest new ideas and have these open new vistas of productivity and performance. We can also reflect and build on these experiences to ensure that they are even more meaningful to our lives. Behaviours towards others and the way we respond to the world can manifest themselves in new and different responses. An example might be that through adverse experiences we can build resilience so that the next negative experience isn't as traumatic and we accept it for what it is. Experiences also teach us new behaviours on a very physical level — if you burn yourself once on a flame you learn not to do it again (hopefully).

The impact of human experiences can also be shared in groups and societies. Firstly, let's examine some group dynamics that can be affected by human experiences. Groups share experiences and adapt and develop behaviours that impact on the group as a whole. Think about the notorious 'bonding' sessions sporting teams have that unite them in a common goal. Think about the behaviours of various gangs in our society. We see plenty of examples of this on American television where gangs based on ethnicity and social groupings form specific sets of behaviours that impact on how they interact with each other and the world. These groupings carry assumptions about how they see the world and respond to it. For example, they may have generally negative reactions to law enforcement and this is ingrained into their codes of behaviour. They are suspicious of the world and the people in it — dividing them up into threats, the law and victims. These behaviours are often reinforced by group experiences such as the initiation rituals which are integral to membership.

Often the impact of these behaviours is to perpetuate stereotypes that then categorise the individuals within these groups. The graphic I have included here shows a stereotypical gang member with the suspicious gaze, ubiquitous hoody and scruffy look. These stereotypes reject new ideas and maintain assumptions about the world, often to the detriment of their members. The experiences they have reinforce their own stereotypical way of viewing anything outside the safety of the group and the cycle continues. Of course, other groups have more positive impacts and see the world as a  very different place and their experiences are designed to be positive interactions. Think about groups such as Rotary who are constructive in the community. Other groups have specialty interests such as Animal Welfare, Surf Lifesaving and charities.

Normal social interactions impact groups and individuals, but it takes a major event to alter the behaviours of whole societies, especially so in the modern world where societies are large in scale. Earlier in human history smaller experiences could alter the behaviour of societies as they were insignificant in size compared to modern ones. We often fail to remember that many of these ancient societies' behaviours were impacted by superstition, religions and cultural habituation. The modern society as we know it is only a recent phenomenon. Just a few hundred years ago with church rule people were forced to think in a specific

way and punished for not adhering to a theological culture. Think of the Spanish Inquisition, the imprisonment of Galileo and other such restrictions on freedom of thought; scientific breakthroughs were hidden or declared witchcraft. Even recently the world has seen societies kept repressed by failed ideologies. The brutality of such regimes has left deep scars on the social psyche of nations as they try to recover. This has had an impact on the human experiences of whole populations, and societies respond accordingly.

One example might be at the conclusion of the Communist regime in East Germany when the Berlin Wall was destroyed as a visual symbol of the new-found freedom of a whole population of people who had been repressed for decades by a brutal and ever-present regime. Many citizens who had grown up in this system, where you could 'disappear' without trial or real evidence, found the idea that you could express yourself incredible. Many of the

East Germans couldn't believe that this freedom was real and that the Stasi (the secret police) were gone.

Other experiences can affect societies in extreme ways. Think about wars and the impact they have on civilian populations.

Climatic events such as earthquakes change the way that people behave and respond to situations. Catastrophic flooding occurred in the US city of New Orleans in 2005. The US President's response to help was not immediate and the national administration was severely criticised for lack of effective action.

Societies also respond to perceived problems such as pollution. In 1989 the oil tanker Exxon Valdez ran aground in Prince William Sound, Alaska with disastrous results. The effects of this event are still being experienced thirty years later.

Societies can be divided, as we saw with the election of Donald Trump in the United States of America and the reaction of the Political Left.

The impact of human experiences on societies can be quite dramatic, as we have seen, while other experiences (such as an election) can go by without a murmur from societies, no matter who wins. As a last thought before we move on you should also consider the impact of the media on societies in the modern world, and how they influence individuals, societies and the development of ideas.

Problems With Human Behaviour

So far, we have discussed the impact of human experiences on behaviour. Now we can begin to develop some more complex judgements and understandings about the impact of those experiences on human behaviours. In simplistic terms it could be assessed as:

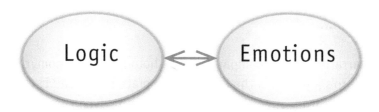

These two opposites on the continuum certainly shape the manner in which we see incidents and how they affect the experience. For instance, if someone you love has no interest in you, it creates a very different reaction to someone you don't care about having no interest in you. It is generally agreed that humans respond more strongly with emotion than they do with logic. Often, it is only through time and reflection that we can understand how an experience has changed and/or altered the manner in which we see a situation or individual.

The Role of Storytelling in Human Experiences

Storytelling has been part of the human experience since 'people' began communicating and it is a method used to convey information and experience as well as be entertaining. Earliest myths were all oral and then people began to write down stories so they weren't lost in time. From this, various theories have developed around storytelling and one is the 'monomyth', which is a template across cultures for storytelling. Let's have a look at this below.

'In narratology and comparative mythology, the monomyth, or the hero's journey, is the common template of a broad category of tales that involve a hero who goes on an adventure, and in a decisive crisis wins a victory, and then comes home changed or transformed.

The concept was introduced in *The Hero with a Thousand Faces* (1949) by Joseph Campbell, who described the basic narrative pattern as follows:

"A hero ventures forth from the world of common day into a region of supernatural wonder: fabulous forces are there encountered and a decisive victory is won: the hero comes back from this mysterious adventure with the power to bestow boons on his fellow man."

Campbell and other scholars, such as Erich Neumann, describe narratives of Gautama Buddha, Moses, and Christ in terms of the monomyth. Critics argue that the concept is too broad or general to be of much use in comparative mythology. Others say that the hero's journey is only a part of the monomyth; the other part is a sort of different form, or colour, of the hero's journey.

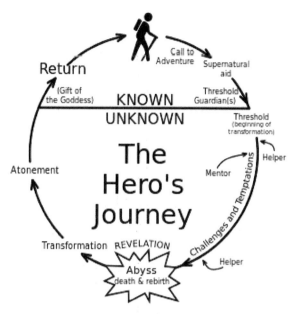

Storytelling in History and its Purpose in Human Experience

Storytelling in oral form was accompanied by some theatrics to make the stories as entertaining as possible. Many of the early narratives were based upon religious ceremonies and stories of the creation of the earth and people(s). As time moved on, these stories were accompanied by dance, music and / or theatre and often were part of lengthy rituals, often taking days. These stories were designed to bring meaning to people's lives by explaining their own existence and the purpose / meaning of life in a time when life expectancy was short and entertainment was scarce. Of course stories were also recorded as these experiences were significant to all people and these stories run across all cultures. Before writing, stories were recorded in pictures such as cave art, in tattoo designs on skin and in designs such as rock piles and the giant carved heads of Easter Island.

Writing changed the manner in which stories were told and many of the old oral traditions were lost, barely being kept alive by specialists. Stories began to travel across cultural and national boundaries on whatever surface could be created. Papyrus, bones, pottery, skins, paper and in more modern times film, video and digital storage have changed, over time, the way in which stories of human experience have been told and shared. Content evolved from myth, fable and legend to history, personal narratives and commentary. Modern narrative form often has an educational or didactic element and can drift into propaganda. Stories of self-revelation can be instructive and give audiences the opportunity to apply learning to individual lives, whereas historically narrative was used in this way for societies and groups as a whole. In recent times narratives have become interactive and audiences can choose how the narrative unfolds.

Whatever form the story takes we all have a seemingly innate need for narratives to make sense of our lives. They either confirm our world view or alter our world view depending on the experience they convey and the experiences that we bring to the narrative. We need to remember that narratives are important to human experience and have been significant since the beginning of time.

The Text as an Experience

The concept of the text as an experience is one area to consider as we look at *Texts and Human Experiences*. Reading or viewing the text is an experience in itself and when we do this we bring our own history (experiences) to the text and this helps shape our understanding.

Think about the personal perspective that you bring to a text. What are some of your experiences that might influence how you read a particular text? Some texts, especially personal narratives of trial and tribulation or loss, can be confronting to some audiences and bring back strong opinions or emotions. Many texts attempt to do this as they convey a particular point of view about the world.

Does what you bring to the text affect what you learn from that text? We also need to delve into how the narrative experience is conveyed and how this in turn impacts upon the manner in which the story is received by audiences across different cultures. For example, Western films where heroes fight Islamic terrorism may well be viewed very differently by audiences in Western democracies and Islamic countries. Even seemingly innocuous narratives like the movie 'The Red Pill' which is about men's rights and created by a woman, has caused a polarisation of views wherever it has been shown. Strong personal experiences and viewpoints certainly bring their own understandings to texts.

Questions for Texts and Human Experiences

- Define the module in your own words.
- How are people connected by shared experiences?
- How might physical experience(s) change the way you respond to the world?
- How do you think a person's context and prior experiences shape how they perceive the world?
- Are experiences unique or do prior experiences have an impact on a current experience and way of seeing life?
- What is positive about human experiences?
- Discuss what is negative about human experiences.
- To what extent does experience shape the way we see other people and / or groups?
- Is an individual's culture part of their experience or is it something else?
- Is it possible not to have any meaningful experiences at all?
- Why do people tell stories?
- What do you think you might learn from a narrative?

WHY STUDY POETRY?

Poetry is a part of life and is about life. It deals with all the emotions of life: love, death, nature, friendship, feelings of pain, anger, frustration – all the moods and ideas that are part of the human condition. Poetry appeals to our understanding through our imagination, making us see what the poet has seen, hear what the poet has heard and experience his feelings. This is particularly true of Slessor with his use of the senses and time to convey human experiences in a meaningful manner.

Useful Literary Terms

Familiarity with the following terms of figurative language, poetic device and technique will enable you to convince your examiner that you have acquired the vocabulary necessary to discuss how the composer attempts to share his ideas through the use of his poetic craft. Remember this is an outcome of your course!

Alliteration	repetition of initial consonant sounds close together – for a special / poetic sound effect / emphasis (e.g. "one summer's evening soaked").
Allusion	a reference to something from history, literature, religion that adds to its meaning
Analysis	to examine closely, take apart for the purpose of greater understanding.
Assonance	repetition of vowel sounds in words or lines close together.

Cliché	word or phrase which is very common and overused.
Climax	where emotions / ideas reach their peak (often the end of a poem).
Criticism	evaluation of literature, finding strong points which support the meaning, looking at style and language use.
Dissonance	harsh sounding words together for a special effect and emphasis.
Enjambment	run-on-lines, with no punctuation pauses, having effect on the sense of the lines in the poem
Free verse	a disregard for traditional rhyme / rhythm rules
Hyperbole	exaggeration for effect / emphasis (eg. 'millionth person').
Imagery	figures of speech –metaphors, similes etc. that make word pictures, comparisons or contrasts, to aid understanding
Irony	a reversal of expected ideas used to make an effect, to draw attention to a point.
Juxtaposition	two contrasting ideas close together for dramatic effect and emphasis

Lyric	a poem that expresses emotions and ideas.
Metaphor	a direct comparison between two things, referring to one in terms of another - without using 'like' or 'as'
Mood	overall emotional effect / feeling set in a line or stanza of a poem.
Motif	dominant theme / object that comes up several times in a poem or collection of poems
Narrative	style of writing which relates a story
Onomatopoeia	words that imitate sound being described, used for the sound effect and emphasis (eg. "whirred with an insect nervousness").
Paradox	a contradiction which actually is true
Personification	to give human qualities to non-living things (eg. "all the sun's disciples cloaked")
Realism	make vividly real by careful attention to detail
Satire	criticise by means of subtle ridicule, with comic effect

Simile	comparison used to describe something more vividly, using 'like' or 'as', to get a certain meaning across
Stanza	divisions within a poem, similar to paragraphs in prose.
Structure	the shape or form of a poem, the way it hangs together
Style	interplay of structure / language / tone that supports the theme
Symbol	an image that stands for a complex idea
Theme	central message / meaning of a piece of writing (eg. memory)
Tone	overall attitude conveyed by the writing to the audience through the combination of subject, mood and style
Transferred epithet	figurative language where an idea is passed from one thing onto another for dramatic immediacy

Theme / Idea

Theme or idea is an important aspect of any literature. Try always to find the idea in a poem, in other words, the *central thread that runs through it* that gives it its unique meaning. Often the title of the poem is the key to its meaning, so look there first. The title of a poem, or story or film is not decided on a whim – the composer puts a great deal of thought into it, and thus to appreciate the text one should give good thought to the title, and any sub-title.

Remember that the poet is presenting his ideas, feelings and arguments about life as he sees it. The reader has to work these out, and different readers may come up with different interpretations, and we may never know for certain exactly what the poet's meaning is. Reading poetry can become very subjective (personal) as the reader recognises feelings and sympathises with the ideas, but poetry analysis must show the interpretation is underpinned at all times by the text itself.

Style

Poetry is a particular and special literary art form, and it is the style of writing that makes it different from the prose of novels. The reader should pay attention to the method of writing because a good poet will be very deliberate about this. There are many formal poetic devices that have been used down the ages to express a poet's ideas and emotions (rhyme, rhythm, language, punctuation etc). Modern poetry is not as disciplined as, for instance, a sonnet by Shakespeare which was limited to 14 lines and a distinct rhyme scheme.

However, that does not mean that there is no 'style' to the poetry. It just may not be obvious at first – but it needs to be found through close scrutiny. Refer to the literary terms above and see what has been used and how the poet has used it to convey his theme, look at the stanza divisions, note the punctuation, pick up the sound effects of alliteration and assonance. Remember that the manner in which the poet does his work is as important as the meaning.

Outlined here are some of Dobson's stylistic features. Find your own examples from the poems for each and note them in the space provided.

1.   Dobson was inspired by art and so uses ekphrastic concepts in many of her poems.

_____

_____

_____

_____

_____

_____

2.   Tight form – Dobson often uses very regular rhyme scheme, rhythm patterns and cyclic structure

_____

_____

_____

_____

_____

_____

3. Comment on the use of the poetic device – imagery in the work of Dobson.

    _____

    _____

    _____

    _____

    _____

    _____

4. Read the quote below and assess it in terms of human experience in the poetry.

    > 'The poems in _Collected_ offer something more than
    > the usual record of a progression. To read them is
    > to follow a quiet mind, but an acute one, through
    > a writing life that over the decades is increasingly
    > responsive to what is near at hand and to the
    > oddness as well as the grandeur of things.'

    http://www.smh.com.au/entertainment/books/an-eternity-in-the-ordinary-20120530-1zjou.html

    _____

    _____

    _____

    _____

    _____

    _____

    _____

5. Metaphor is used to enhance mood and atmosphere as well as to represent the complex themes relating to time, life and death.

    _____

    _____

    _____

    _____

    _____

    _____

    _____

6. The website below is a retrospective on Dobson's work and is highly illuminating on aspects of her style and development. Make a note of some of the comments on style that will assist you in your study of the poems. It also discusses some of the experiences which had an impact on her poetry.

    http://www.nla.gov.au/sites/default/files/rosemary_dobson.pdf

    _____

    _____

    _____

    _____

    _____

    _____

    _____

7.   'Dobson's poetry divides into three broad periods. The earliest period begins with her first volume of poetry, In a Convex Mirror (1944), and ends in her mid-30s with Child with a Cockatoo (1955). Cock Crow (1965) represents a middle period and Over the Frontier (1978) marks the beginning of her later period.'

http://www.theaustralian.com.au/arts/review/rosemary-dobsons-poetic-life-in-pursuit-of-the-intervening-angel/news-story/27b95e80957092281fb4346d49f19254

How might these stages of life change the style of her poetry?

_____

_____

_____

_____

_____

_____

_____

_____

_____

_____

_____

_____

_____

_____

_____

THE COMPOSER – ROSEMARY DOBSON

While background on composers can help you understand the poems set for study, be aware that examiners will expect you to engage closely with the actual poem(s) and find the relevance to human experiences.

Rosemary Dobson was born in Sydney in 1920. Her father, Arthur Dobson, was an English engineer. Her grandfather, Austin Dobson, was an acclaimed English poet although Rosemary was not aware of his achievements until she was eleven. This was after she had written her first poems. (She began to write poetry at seven.)

Rosemary's father died when she was just five years old, leaving her mother Marjorie to raise Rosemary and her older sister Ruth. When Rosemary was nine, an aunt on her father's side visited. Due to connections, Marjorie was offered a live-in 'house mistress' position at Frensham School in Mittagong. At first the school would only take one of her daughters so Marjorie rejected the offer, but a subsequent offer, which included schooling for both daughters, was accepted.

Rosemary Dobson remained at the progressive Winifred West school, Frensham, for the entirety of her schooling. At seventeen, Dobson self-published her first book of poems. She stayed on at the school as an assistant to the Art teacher, and worked with another staff assistant called Joan Phipson, who had also been a student at the school. Phipson became an award winning Australian children's writer. Phipson set up Frensham Press and it was on this press that Dobson's first collection of poems was printed. Phipson and even the Woolfs, with their Hogarth Press in

London, were influences in Dobson's life as she became involved in the process of not only writing, but proofing and printing.

Rosemary Dobson received an inheritance from her grandfather which she used to finance a move to Sydney and attendance at Sydney University. She took classes in English, Art and Design. The renowned Australian painter Thea Proctor taught her drawing. Elegance, strength, discrimination and balance were important factors which Dobson saw in Proctor's work and which she saw as relevant in the creation of her own poetry. Critics later validated and discussed these qualities in her poetry.

When she was twenty-one Dobson got a job as a proof reader with Sydney publishers Angus and Robertson. Her first professionally published book of poetry, In a Convex Mirror, came out in 1944. In 1948 she won the Sydney Morning Herald prize for poetry. Further publications followed: The Ship of Ice (1948), Child with a Cockatoo (1955) and Cock Crow (1965) and so on through the years until the 1991 'Collected Poems'. The poems selected by NESA give a broad picture of her work over the years and cover her thoughts on human experiences. You will find much to offer for your studies in these poems.

In 1952, Rosemary married Alec Bolton, a fellow-employee of Angus and Robertson. They had three children. Between 1966 and 1971, they lived in London while Alec ran the editorial department of Angus and Robertson. They returned to Australia in 1971 because they wanted their children to grow up Australian. Rosemary wrote little poetry during their time in London but she was able to travel in Europe and enhance her love and knowledge of art. Her ekphratic poems reference many great works of art.

Alec began work in Canberra at the National Library in 1971. He set up Brindabella Press and Rosemary worked with him as an editor and proof reader. In 1996, Alec Bolton died. Rosemary Dobson was honoured with the Order of Australia in 1987. She also won the Patrick White Award for poetry. She is remembered as a highly regarded Australian poet who received many accolades and awards and went on to publish hundreds of poems. She published sixteen volumes of poetry in her lifetime. Dobson died in Canberra in 2012, aged 92. Her writing spanned over seventy years.

CONTEXT

Literary / Historical Context

Rosemary Dobson (1920–2012) is said to have had a life-long interest in European culture, especially the paintings of the masters. This interest is reflected in some of her poems set for study. Elizabeth Lawson claimed Dobson's early painting poems, poems which make intertextual reference to the work of painters, "concern the capacity of art to speak across centuries into the reader's present with fresh immediacy." This quote highlights human experiences, an aspect of which in the poems produced in one context and form, can be reinvented to speak to new audiences. This idea is captured in the words,

> *Old Painting and old poems*
> *Find distant destinations*
> *Can seed new songs*
> *In another language.*

Translations under the Trees
(Lawson in *Rosemary Dobson a Celebration* ed. Joy Hooton for Friends of the National Library Australia, Canberra 2000.)

Consider these ideas and align them with the technique of ekphrasis (writing based on artwork) when looking at some set poems.

Throughout her life, Dobson lived in close contact with other creative people – artists, poets and authors of all kinds. Her own work blossomed in this context. Whilst never wavering in her sense of herself as an Australian, her art always looked to Europe as a source of inspiration. Rosemary Dobson was interested in exploring the relationship between Australia and its European influences. Her work is said to examine the balance between dualities – the past and the present, consistency and variety, tradition and innovation, culture and the mundane, reserve and passion, light and dark, myth and reality and the relation of all of these dualities to the 'duality' of Australia and Europe.

You may well develop your own thoughts regarding human experiences in the set poems and remember that all of these go directly to human experiences that she is investigating. Dobson's use of juxtaposition or balanced contrast, points towards "human qualities and emotions", a phrase from the Texts and Human Experiences rubric. You are well advised to incorporate the rubric into your response and ensure you use this study guide to complement rather than replace your own engagement with the set poems. Does Australia stand for the present, variety, innovation, passion, the mundane and reality in these dualities and Europe for the past, consistency, tradition, reserve, culture, and myth? Or is it even more complex than this? Where are the human experiences that Dobson shares with us through the poems set for study?

We will look to Dobson's poetry for answers.

'YOUNG GIRL AT A WINDOW'

Glossary

latch	A device for holding consisting basically of a bar falling or sliding into a catch or groove.
mortal	Something that is subject to death, a transitory life, belonging to this world.
thresholds	The entrance to a house or building. In this instance it can also be any place or point of entering or beginning.
guiltless	A person who is free from guilt i.e. innocent or in the poem it can also mean having no knowledge or experience.
sheaves	Bundles in which cereal plants or crops are bound after harvest.

Poem Analysis

This three stanza poem was published in 1944 in, In a Convex Mirror. Dobson was twenty four at the time of publication. It is addressed to a young girl who is physically looking out of a window and metaphorically 'looking out at life'. It may well seem that she is on the threshold of many experiences.

The girl is urged, "Lift your hand to the window latch". This instruction is forcing the girl to consider, at least, opening the latch of the window. Is this to better see out, to remove the barrier of the window that lies between the young girl and life? Whatever the reason for the advice, it is not taken and the persona, "Sighing", decides to, "turn and move away". The girl does not open the window. It is suggestive here that to have any experience you need to approach life and we wonder why the girl refrains from opening the window into the wider world.

The reference to the crossing of "mortal swords" is a reference to conflict, and is usually seen in a Biblical or medieval context. The important thing here, however, is the ambiguity of "crossed'" – swords might be crossed, but so are thresholds. The young girl is about to cross a threshold. The window ledge serves as a liminal space, symbolising the potential for new experiences.

"The fading air is stained with red" could be a reference to the sunset, as it fades and is red in colour. It might also suggest menstruation. In the next line, though, it definitely becomes a reference to the colour of blood. It makes physical the abstract notion of the killing of Time.

Time is repeated into the first line of the second stanza: "Or Time was lost." In the clock on the wall, "the guiltless minute hand is still", suggesting that time has stopped. Thus, the minute hand is "guiltless" as it is not contributing to the passing of time and its accompanying decay. This is an attempt to hold the moment, to defeat Time. This sense of entrapment, of Time and of childhood within the room is reflected in the tight structure and regular rhyme scheme of the poem.

The room and the light are both personified and then made "hosts to you this final night." The word "final" suggests, again that something is ending: that the young girl is on a threshold of some sort. Presumably this is the threshold between girlhood and womanhood and between childhood and adulthood. This is the human experience that is a collective one and while this girl's experience is purely her the concept of this divide is certainly common and part of the collective memory.

The image of the clock is picked up in "the gently-turning hills" that replace the turning of the minute hand. The girl sees her life spread out before her as seen in the quotation, "Travel a journey with your eyes / In forward footsteps." This is about time, which can only move forward, not back. "This way", that is, in a forward direction, "the map of living lies." The poem then ends with a focus beyond the entrapment of the room and towards the imagined future.

"And this the journey you must go" – the key word is "must". It is the human condition; we have no choice regarding the journey. Life's journey will be, "Through grass and sheaves and, lastly, snow." The images of "grass and sheaves" are images of fertility and growth, while "snow" is the image for winter, a season with connotations of hardship and death.

It has been said that this poem reads as though it may have been based on a painting. This is a definite possibility as Dobson used inter-textual references to artworks in other poems. Whether this is the case or not, the work of art, the painting or the poem, gives the moment a permanence that a real girl, of course, would not have. The text has frozen and metaphorically killed Time, but the girl's destiny is in the final symbolic line of the poem – "and, lastly, snow". This is the metaphoric winter of life and she must journey on towards it.

This may be an ekphrastic poem, (An **ekphrastic poem** is a vivid description of a scene or, more commonly, a work of art. Through the imaginative act of narrating and reflecting on the "action" of a painting or sculpture, the **poet** may amplify and expand its meaning.) based on possible art works titled Girl at the Window or Girl at a Window or even, Young Woman at a Window, by European artists including, Dali (1925), Cassatt (1883–4), Gauguin (1888) Greuze (1725–1805), Rembrandt (1651) or even Vermeer. Whether based on an art work or not, Dobson shares with these artists the capture and preservation of a moment through the creation of a text. The adjective 'young' or the word 'girl' in the title suggests there are looming discoveries to be made in life's journey.

There is a duality upon which this poem is based – the capturing of moments in time through art and the written word and the transience of human life. This is a recurring theme in Dobson's work and is significant in that, through capturing a moment, it can be rediscovered by subsequent generations.

The Poem and Human Experiences

The poem is about a young girl who is reticent (meaning hesitant) to move outside the known, to discover life. The "window" in the first line represents a barrier between the girl and the world outside and its experiences. Her decision not to open the window "turn and move away" indicates her unwillingness to discover what is out in the world.

The girl is obviously having a personal experience. The reference to "mortal swords" is a reference to conflict and danger, and implies a threat she is not prepared to face. She remains, "On thresholds at the end of day" unwilling to cope with the conflict this experience will cause in her life.

The references to time in the first and second stanzas, "Time was killed" and "...Time was lost" indicate that she is doing all she can to stop this change in her life and the personal discoveries that will accompany it. In the case of art, it alludes to the permanence of art as time is preserved yet reminds the responder that some things cannot be experienced.

The repetition of "time" and the personification in "time was killed" indicates an attempt to stop the inevitable change that is coming in life. This is an attempt to hold on to childhood, to defeat time and avoid the changes and the discoveries that adulthood will bring in the persona's life.

This idea is further developed by the personification of "The watchful room" which is host to her "this final night." The word "final" implies that the girl's childhood is ending and she fears the changes that becoming a woman will bring. Thus, she fears the changes which lead to self-discovery. The personification also highlights the gentle tone of the poem as other humans seem to have let the girl down. The fact that inanimate objects become her hosts and, ..."nobody spoke and nobody will", highlights that this process of maturation and journeying through life's seasons is a journey of experience which is taken alone. Some experiences cannot be avoided no matter how hard an individual tries. "And this the journey you must go / Through..." The key word used here is "must"- the young girl must take this journey, and make the changes and experiences associated with the journey. She cannot avoid the human condition and will travel,

"Through grass and sheaves and, lastly snow."

This imagery represents the seasons of the year and of life. It can relate to the aging process. She has discovered, through her experiences, that change cannot be avoided. Thus, Dobson is suggesting that in order to have a significant experience one must be prepared to take risks and change and this may well be a solitary journey. There is an implicit understanding that the process of human experiences, as seen in the poem, brings with it positive ramifications such as new understandings and renewed perceptions. The girl's experience may be projected onto your own life as, like the subject, you stand at a similar transformative threshold, that of adulthood.

Questions for 'Young Girl at a Window'

1. What does the window represent in this poem?

2. What is associated with time in this poem?

3. Why is time an important image in this poem?

4. Why do you think the young girl avoids opening the window in the poem?

5. How does the poet suggest the young girl is trying to avoid making changes in her life?

6. How does the poet suggest the young girl will be unable to avoid making changes in her life?

7. What have you learnt about human experience in this poem? Write a paragraph supporting your ideas with close reference to the poem.

8. Suggested activity. Find a copy of Hopkins' poem, 'Spring and Fall' and a copy of John Keats' poem, 'Ode on a Grecian Urn'. What similarities regarding the human experience can be made when compared with Dobson's poem? What is the tone, or the composer's attitude, in each poem?

9. Look up some of the listed art works with similar titles. Do you think the poem may be based on a painting? Justify your answer with close reference to the poem and incorporate the term *ekphratic* in your response.

10. Complete your Reading Journal sheet/sheets for this poem.

'OVER THE HILL'

Glossary

dredges	Means to clear out usually references as to the bottom of a river but here it can also more meaningfully apply to unearth something or bring something to notice.
roan	A colour normally associated with horses of the colour sorrel, chestnut or bay, sprinkled with grey or white
insolence	Rude in a contemptuous manner usually through behaviour or speech

Poem Analysis

This poem explores the experience of aging. The title is a literal reference to the progress of the character but obviously is also a well-known expression of being old, and perhaps 'past it'. It uses the journey of a workman home at the end of the day to reflect the experience of aging and the latent power of the aged.

The poem begins with a description of a workmen returning home after the day's work. "This workman" seems to drag himself home at the end of the work day. The workman seems tired as he "dredges" himself home, implying that he is dragging his feet. His "bluntly forward boots" present his dogged progress. He seems so fixed on his arrival home that the earth sprays behind him. Yet, he seems a giant and is impacting upon the earth as he moves. There is even a sense of carelessness as he powers home. The "swung cap scooping cups of wind" hints of a latent power which is further reflected in the comment that he "fills the sky". It is not a weak figure. Yet it is the end of the day and the "windows facing west" refer to the setting of the sun. Despite this, he still appreciates the beauty of the landscape which is captured in the attractive image of the "lemon-coloured light" as the night comes on.

It is at this point that there seems to be an alternative for the workmen. He is not restricted by the day's end. He can choose to make another journey instead of passively looking at the end of the day. With huge dimensions that allow him to loom over the land and reach the moon, he might be striding "from hill to hill". This is a more energetic and imaginative experience which is hinted at by the aside which has him using the moon as a hat hook. Here the aside is a clever understatement that emphasises his power. Like the journey home, there is an image of latent energy as he lights his pipe – not as a rebellious teen but with the carelessness that comes with maturity. It is the genuine disregard for public opinion built on the confidence of experience.

The potential of the workman is captured in the line, "He could move mountains if he cared" but it is clear that he does not. Here the wisdom born of experience is reflected in the line,

> *But a mountain in the palm of one's hand*
> *Is a troublesome thing*

It is not laziness or even powerlessness that keeps him from being heroic or adventurous but a realisation that calm responses are often the best. Certainly the poem ends on a quiet note, where the workman, despite is energetic striding and ability to do the incredible feat of mountain moving, just lets things be.

The Poem and Human Experiences

Taken metaphorically, the workman can be seen to personify the process of aging. His movement home at the end of the day can be seen to represent the human experience of aging and movement towards death. The use of the word "this" hints that it may be Dobson herself. Indeed, the power of the character may well be a comment on the power of the artist to affect the world. Perhaps she is using the poem to explore her own experience of being a craftsman moving toward the end of her career.

The most important thing is to realise that the image the audience receives of maturing is not one of weakness. The image of the workman striking the match is full of masculine, heroic power. Dobson intends to represent the aged as carefree and with influence. There may be a sense of tiredness in the beginning of the poem but it develops into a sense of calm wisdom. The "striding" symbolises the capacity for action and creativity. The workman appreciates nature and beauty. Unlike the rebellious, hasty actions of ignorant youth, the persona chooses not to act because it is less "troublesome". It might be a quiet existence that is desired but it is a preference that respects others. This is shown in the reverential image of the workman treating the mountain with care as he "quiets the trees". There is real sense of awareness of others and repercussions.

There is an acceptance of the coming of the end but it is accompanied by a positive image of aging. Through the image of the workman, this natural cycle of life is shown to be one of latent power, wisdom and the awareness of ramifications beyond the self.

Questions for 'Over the Hill'

1. In your own words, explain what is happening in this poem on a plot level.

2. Why is it important to Dobson's message about the human experience that the workman is larger than life?

3. The poem positions the audience as an observer, somewhat detached from this scene. How does that contribute to our feelings towards the workman?

4. Explain how your answer to 3 above makes the message of the comments about the human experience more effective.

5. Explain the effect of the aside on the audience in the poem. Why has Dobson included it? Think how it makes you feel.

6. How is the natural environment represented in the poem? What is the comment through this about the workman?

7. The poem has a sense of immediacy. Trace how this is achieved and the effect it has on the effectiveness of the poem.

8. Make a list of all the symbols in the poem. You can start with dusk – the end of a day, representing the end of a life...

9. The workman is male yet it has been suggested the poem is about the poet's experience and power. Why might Dobson have chosen to use a male figure?

10. Complete your Reading Journal sheet/sheets for this poem.

'SUMMER'S END'

Glossary

miraculous	Like a miracle; performed by or involving supernatural powers. A person with the power to work miracles.
indolent	Slothful, lazy, someone or thing that avoids work or exertion.
recedes	To move away from, to retreat, to become more distant
abandoned	To be left, forsaken or deserted. Also to be uncontrolled or uninhibited – utterly lacking moral constraints.
bitter	Harsh and disagreeable, hard to bear, admit or accept. People can be characterised by intense antagonism or hostility.
ambush	to act from a position of concealment, attack by surprise
slander	A malicious, false and defamatory statement either oral or in print.
resentfully	The feeling of displeasure or indignation at some act, remark, person etc. regarded as causing injury or insult

Poem Analysis

Summer's End is a poem in two parts. Each is concerned with very popular recreational events in Australia.

1.   *After the Summer Season* tells of the end of the beach break whereas

2.   *Picnic* is about a picnic by a water way, more in the bush.

It is important that each tell of the end of the experience. The poem is both nostalgic and positive about the memories being recalled and the sensuality of each.

1. After the Summer Season

This first part tells of the end of the summer season. The colder "winter" waters are depicted as powerfully sweeping away ("in a flood") the paraphernalia of the summer beach season. The movement of people away from the beach, back to to their real homes is depicted in a metaphor of a wave. Taken away to the solid "tramline" and the "dignified bus" the people are caught up in "the foam and splash of departure". There is a sense of speed, powerlessness and confusion. The cumulative listing of the "sunhats", "surfboards", "scarves", "sunshades", even the people on the beach, adds to the power of the wave. This is emphasised by the repetition of "and" and the alliteration of the "s" sound. The sentences are long and build to a crescendo of energy indicated by the dash after "indolent sleepers". This suggests an abrupt awakening, just like when one is caught out by an unexpected wave on a beach. The present tense adds immediacy and contributes to the hurrying pace of the verse. The poetry implies all are caught up in the change of the seasons and are powerless to stop their movements away now the season is finished.

Continuing the image of the wave, the very indented line, "Then from the roadway…" mimics the receding wave as it pulls back "with a sigh" and the beach area is quiet and calm without the tourists and holiday makers. Rooms are "shuttered" and, like the flies, all settles to inactivity. The cat is restless and is forced to hunt outside. Another indented line adds to the dislocating and eerie silence of the beach with a walker who seems misplaced. The walking of a person on the beach is said to be abnormal by likening her to "the lonely mermaid / Who married a mortal". Here it is suggested that the only one left at the beach is not meant to be there. Out of place and unhappy, it is only love that keeps such a person in a place when all have gone.

2. Picnic

Seemingly unconnected this second part of the poem deals with another recreational experience. It is another snapshot of the end of the summer season. It is autumn and in this section the past tense emphasises the fire is over and time is moving on. As a contrast to the first part, it is the fire that signifies the change to maturity.

This is a more personal section; the persona speaks in first person of losing the self to memory, "Dreaming by the fire". It is a memory of high definition where the detail adds to the power of the nostalgic vision. The many adjectives paint a vivid scene and it is clear the persona has very strong recollections. The aside "(years and years ago)" is included to add more emphasis to the pervasiveness of the recollection. The ellipsis adds a tone of whimsy and suggests the persona might have continued on and on. The energy of the youth has been captured in the energy of the twig boats and tadpoles. The power of the memory is further shown by, "I was a child again" where the high modality and certain tone. These are youthful experiences easily identified with, and Dobson cleverly includes the audience in the fond recollections.

The final lines are paradoxical as the persona "called myself" back to the present. Here, "watching / For a child to run back through Time" shows how embroiled the persona is in the memory of the past.

Links to Texts and Human Experiences

Both sections of this poem deal with the passing of time. Each depict the end of a cycle. The beach culture is forced to give way to the seasons which represent the tides of life. Here the wave image is a very common image associated with the flow and ebb of time. The people on the beach, best shown by the "indolent sleepers" are passive and cannot resist. They are channelled back to their lives as is right. The energy of the earlier summer has been transformed and absorbed into the change of seasons. The rightness of this progression of time seems to be shown through the image of the mermaid. Time and change cannot be escaped. The attempt at it is not successful but shown to be a sad, painful failure.

The second part also shows the cycle of change and passing of time. Here the persona may lose herself to memory – a memory that is as energetic as it is cool and pleasant – yet she must call herself back. Perhaps there is a resentment to the effect of time depicted in the, "Savour of sadness". You may see some violence in the smoke fighting with the "crossed blades of sunlight". Here the fire appears to be reasserting itself, "Detecting an ambush" and making the billy black and "bubbling with anger". These lines seem to suggest the insistence of the burning. It seems to represent time as it is only "in the gully" – away from the fire in the cool that the past can be clutched onto.

The progression from summer to autumn and the obvious next stage to winter is a fairly common image of a life cycle. While the autumn is traditionally representing old age, winter is usually death. Both these sections are in the autumn and point to the progression of time. The second part quite obviously links to the stages in life and some may see the image of the persona, lost in a dream at the end to represent dying. No matter how you see the end of the poem, there is a sense of lost youth and the passing of time.

Questions for 'Summer's End'

1. In your own words, explain what is happening in this poem on a plot level.

2. The winter is seen as cleansing. Explain why this is important.

3. How does the poem's appearance on the page resonate with the events being described?

4. Explain how the enjambment (run on lines) helps contribute to the effect of the poem you described in your answer to 3 above.

5. Identify some aural techniques used by Dobson in Part 1 to echo the sounds of the waves on the beach.

6. How is Part 2 made personal and what is the effect of this on the audience?

7. Part 2 has a reminiscing, dream-like tone to it. Explain how Dobson creates this and why.

8. Make a list of all the emotive language in the poem. You can start with *miraculous*. How is Dobson shaping the audience's response to the two scenes she is representing?

9. Identify the aspects of the poem that make it clearly Australian. To what extent does this limit the wider relevance of her comments about our experiences as humans?

10. Complete your Reading Journal sheet/sheets for this poem.

'THE CONVERSATION'

Glossary

scoured	To clean or purge, usually referred to as cleaning with hard rubbing, scouring to remove debris, impurities or anything undesirable.
bales	 A large bundle or package prepared for shipping, storage and / or sale and usually tightly compressed and secured by wires or the like.
horizon	 The line or circle that forms the apparent boundary between earth and sky.

Poem Analysis

This poem tells of the persona's meeting of an old, mute man one morning. However, while the old man does not actually speak, the poem is an account of what the persona is sure he is saying. Is it a positive poem where the recounted meeting brings the persona joy and a heightened appreciation of life and its potential.

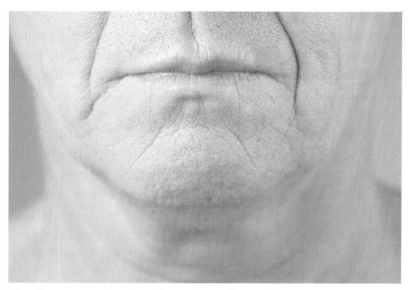

The first stanza begins abruptly as the audience seems to enter the situation 'mid conversation'. This emphasises the energy of the meeting which is exaggerated by the old man's manner of communicating as he "punched into his cap". Very poetically and rather unrealistically, the persona attributes his actions to be a positive acclamation of the environment. The persona interprets his mute action as beautiful description of her imagination. Notably the description is in terms of nature and, specifically, farming. His "old fist like a knotted branch" seems an extension of the natural world as is his craft. He is thought to 'speak' of the land and wool. The processes of teasing and scouring are involved. The audience is to assume he is a farmer. The success of the "full" bales seems to parallel the beauty of the morning with its mist around the hills.

The second stanza is used to show how the persona feels perfectly attuned to the old man. She too, "likewise punched my hat" and used the same wool imagery to respond in kind. The metaphor is extended through reference to further wool processes in "comb and spin", "thread" and "wind". There is an affinity which is emphasised by the certainty about the weather in the future. This is emphasised by the highly modal "will" in "At noonday / The wind will comb and spin..." The two characters are united.

The belief that such a simple action can be interpreted in such a way was always unbelievable. Now, the extension of the imagery reveals this as even more ludicrous. Perhaps Dobson seeks to reveal how communication is flawed by the particular interpretation any individual places on it. The mute old man who speaks with utter simplicity – no words just simple actions, is a huge contrast to the complicated poetic responses that the persona attributes to him.

This idea is shown further in the third stanza which returns to the old man as he 'speaks' again. His gesture "to the horizon" is interpreted as "careless joy". The persona is sure ("I was quick to know") he refers to an exotic adventure, "That over the hills lay China". Of course, this is a ridiculous, far too precise understanding. The juxtaposition is a little silly and amusing. It may well be seen as an acceptance of true limitations in communication. Yet, so too are the possibilities of the world and of travel highlighted by this reference to China.

The memory has remained with the persona and is testament to the power of the image. It was, "Years, years ago" where the repetition of "years" highlights the time gone by but is still represented as energetic and influential. The reference to "Children" reminds the audience of the purity of their perception and appreciations which are uncorrupted by the adult world.

Meanwhile the use of "fools" may well be a Shakespearean reference to the type of fool that has far greater perception than the modern title. Nevertheless, the wisdom of the moment is acknowledged in the final lines, "That excellent old madman / wordless and wise, and I". Here the "I" seems an afterthought and less powerful than the old man who is seen to value nature and the land so much.

Links to Texts and Human Experiences

Many of the links have already been discussed in the textual analysis. However the two main points are listed below.

Here the idea of the importance of a love of the land and nature can be seen. This delight is aligned with wisdom. Appreciation of the natural world is represented as positive and Dobson draws on her own experiences here. Perhaps the connection between the two is Dobson's way of celebrating the beauty of nature and its ability to teach us. The meeting is deemed as important and the farmer as "wise". The two characters are joined by their apparent joy and wonder in nature – of both the land and its bounty. The speaker parallels the man's love of the land and his craft.

The poem also explores our experiences communicating with each other. We are social creatures and value social exchange.

This poem can be seen to hint at the flaws in that communication. Often we think we know exactly what others mean but perhaps we do not at all. The title is ironic as there really is no genuine conversation at all.

Questions for 'The Conversation'

1. In your own words, explain what is happening in this poem on a plot level.

2. Dobson creates a vibrant image of the old man. Describe him, supporting your impression with THREE quotes.

3. What is the effect of starting the poem mid-activity, without a real introduction to orient the audience?

4. Explain how the enjambment (run on lines) contributes to the effect of the poem. Refer to a specific example in your answer.

5. Explain the irony in the title in your own words.

6. Identify the emotive words used to describe the natural environment. Explain how Dobson uses these words, referring to some in particular, to position her audience.

7. Explain how Dobson creates a conversational tone in the poem. What is the effect of this for the audience?

8. There are a number of similes in the poem. List them and explain how they are particularly suited to the topic.

9. It is unlikely the comparisons chosen (see Question 8) are accidents. How do they help Dobson's audience appreciate her comments on the human experience?

10. Complete your Reading Journal sheet/sheets for this poem.

'COCK CROW'

Glossary

absolved	To release or set free from guilt, duty, obligation or release people from blame for the consequences of their actions. Remission of sins.
denied	To state that something declared to be true isn't. To withhold something. To refuse to recognise or acknowledge a person.
illusion	Something that gives a false impression of reality.
thrice	Three times in succession

Poem Analysis

'Dobson's poetry is not as simple as it appears: close reading of "Cock Crow" to show how it plays out various levels of "between" – on the bridge between house and town; between generations; between responsibility and freedom; between being and nonbeing. Biblical allusion to Peter denying Christ; most readings simplify by identifying speaker with Peter. Note that Luke's gospel is unique: "The Lord turned and looked at Peter." (Luke 22:61) Speaker is between Christ and Peter: denied and denying. Note "And I that stood between denied" – at the end of line, "denied" is able to operate as at once passive and active and so generate two levels of meaning.'

https://ninglundecember.files.wordpress.com/2008/05/lecture7.pdf

The title is originally from the Hebrew and refers to the beginning of the day or dawn when the cock traditionally rows. It is also a biblical reference when Jesus prophesied that Peter would betray him thrice (three times) before the cock crowed twice. Mark 14:66-72 is the Bible reference for this story. You can read this below.

Peter Denies Jesus

'**66** And as Peter was below in the courtyard, one of the servant girls of the high priest came, **67** and seeing Peter warming himself, she looked at him and said, "You also were with the Nazarene, Jesus." **68** But he denied it, saying, "I neither know nor understand what you mean." And he went out into the gateway and the rooster crowed. **69** And the servant girl saw him and began again to say to the bystanders, "This man is one of them." **70** But again he denied it. And after a little while the bystanders again said to Peter, "Certainly you are one of them, for you are a Galilean." **71** But he began to invoke a curse on himself and to swear, "I do not know this man of whom you speak." **72** And immediately the rooster crowed a second time. And Peter remembered how Jesus had said to him, "Before the rooster crows twice, you will deny me three times." And he broke down and wept.'

*https://www.biblegateway.com/passage/
?search=Mark+14%3A66-72&version=ESV*

The emphasis on individuality in the poem is established at the beginning of the poem through the speaker desiring to "be myself, alone." She has left other people behind in the "lit house" to spend time by herself with her thoughts. The suggestion is that she is overwhelmed by what is going on in the house and needs to escape. The use of the word "house" rather than home suggests she feels a lack of connection to the place and the people in it at that moment.

"Three times I took that lonely stretch/Three times..." The repetition of "three" could simply suggest that the persona has a lot of troubling thoughts to deal with, but the use of "thrice" in the last stanza suggests she is betraying someone or perhaps even betraying herself through the biblical allusion to Peter's betrayal of Jesus. In leaving the house she has, temporarily at least, escaped her responsibilities "...absolved me of my bonds."

In the third stanza, the responder leaves her mother and daughter in the house, denying them to meet her own need of isolation. She, "...denied/Their needs in shutting the door." The persona's obvious need for isolation and personal space is clear. Dobson, wrote about a woman, both mother and daughter, leaving the house to "escape her bonds." The poet herself commented to McCooey in an interview, that this poem, "expressed the dilemma of the creative person who has human responsibilities that must be met". Dobson noted that it seemed to be an idea that many had overlooked. Such themes are relevant to feminist literary criticism and the conflict between a women's experiences and demands of roles may be explored.

The persona needs solitude to organise her thoughts. Her responsibilities have become too much for her to cope with, they have become a burden to her. Paradoxically, in the fourth stanza, she also acknowledges her deep love for her family; they are a part of her. This is seen in the poignant image, "And love that grows about the bone."

"Too brief illusion!" This phrase indicates that the isolation cannot continue. The exclamation mark indicates the persona's frustration at not being able to continue to be alone and the realisation that she is abdicating her responsibilities. The use of "thrice" in this final stanza rather than three, coupled with the title and the cock crow in the final stanza, establishes the iblical allusion to Peter's betrayal of Jesus. (Mark 14: 66-72). Like Peter the cock had crowed "thrice" as she walked along the road, three times denying her responsibility to her family by refusing to return to the house. In doing so she was able to hold on to the fantasy of her independence.

> And turned the handle of the door
> Thinking I knew his meaning well.

The persona can no longer deny her responsibilities; like Peter she comes to the realization of what she has "thrice" denied. She returns home to meet her responsibilities.

Links to Texts and Human Experiences

There are two main ideas in this poem. The first idea is established at the beginning of the poem in the persona's desire to "be myself alone." The persona of the poem has made a decision that her experiences have impacted negatively on her 'self': that is, she needs to abandon her responsibilities and be alone for a while. She is overwhelmed by her responsibilities. She has no emotional connection at this point to what is going on as indicated by her use of the noun "house" rather than home which is a more emotive term.

The fact that Dobson uses the biblical image of Peter's betrayal of Jesus suggests the persona feels some guilt in leaving her responsibilities behind in the house. In the third stanza responders realise the reason for this guilt; she has left her mother and daughter in the house.

> "My mother and my daughter slept."

In her isolation the persona discovers, paradoxically, that she loves her mother and daughter. She describes the extent of the love in the image, "And that love grows about the bone" but in her guilt there is also the personal discovery that she needs more personal time and isolation, more time to "escape her bonds."

There is another human experience undertaken by the persona in this poem. The realisation is that she cannot remain free of her responsibilities. "Too brief illusion!" The exclamation mark indicates the persona's frustration at having to return to the house and deal with her responsibilities. There is also an acceptance of the responsibilities her mother and daughter represent.

The second main idea involves the personal experiences of the poet. As the previous quote from an interview with Dobson indicates, the personal could be seen as Dobson trying to escape her responsibilities to find the time and space to write. This would create a personal dilemma for a creative person needing the time and space to produce, yet having the responsibilities of a daughter and mother. The existence of the poem indicates that she continues to produce her art, despite her family responsibilities and her frustration regarding the act of creating her art. There is a sense of the persona betraying both herself as an artist and her family within this poem.

Questions for 'Cock Crow'

1. Is Dobson's use of religious imagery effective in this poem? Why or why not?

2. Could the poem be a metaphorical representation of part of Dobson's life? Support your answer with evidence.

3. 3. What is the significance of the poet's use of the word "house" rather than "home"?

4. What experiences does the persona have in this poem?

5. Is the persona of the poem obliged to return to her responsibilities? Why? / Why not? Support your answer with close textual reference to the poem.

6. What have you learnt about human experience in this poem? Write a paragraph supporting your ideas with close reference to the poem.

7. Read Gwen Harwood's 'In the Park'. Compare the two poems and reflect on similarities and differences as they relate to the concept of human experience and familial responsibilities.

8. Complete your Reading Journal sheet/sheets for this poem.

'AMY CAROLINE'

Glossary

Bendigo	Bendigo is a city in Victoria, Australia which is situated in the middle of the state with a population of app. 100,000 people. Founded principally because of gold during the 1850s it was a sheep station prior to that. Gold mining there is still profitable today.
Eaglehawk	Eaglehawk is another gold-mining town in Victoria and it is situated north-west of Bendigo. The gold rush raised its population but now it has about 5,000 residents.
custom	A habitual practice often a collective convention
geraniums	A type of plant of genus pelargonium
meditative	Contemplative, thoughtful, reflection
jinker	An Australian slang term for a sulky

Poem Analysis

This poem is about the persona's grandmother. It is a poem which fondly celebrates this woman's stoic acceptance and continual endurance of her hard life. So too is it a poem which reflects on the position of women and their roles in a patriarchal Australian society. While the grandmother's life was in another time the celebration of her commitment and strength despite her lack of power in her choices still resonates with many women's experiences in modern society.

The poem begins in first person with the possessive, "My". It is a claim to the protagonist in the poem. The use of her name, "Amy Caroline" makes the poem more personal and, like the expression, "Whatever chanced", echoes the grandmother's era by echoing to a past, more formal time. The grandmother is likened to a bird. The image of her holding her head to one side implies intelligence and an appraising approach to life. This is supported by the reference to her "bright eyes". The anecdote of setting the extra place perhaps implies a passive aggressive response to her past life. It represents a determination not to compromise one's values and hints at hidden strength and endurance. It would seem she was not a wealthy woman and lived in a "thin" house. It is not presented as a comfortable house as it "spoke aloud of every kind of weather". This seems to be juxtaposed to a more protective, wholesome country life she used to have.

The grandmother's kindness and warmth is also shown by her care for the natural world: "She put out food for lizards..." and "saved / The household water for geraniums". This positive representation of Amy Caroline is reinforced by the image of her playing the piano. It is a refinement that brings another facet to this admired woman. The reference to her "Perched" might be seen to extend the earlier bird imagery but more likely hints at a sense of discomfort. This is reinforced by her playing in the "semi-dark". You might see this as symbolising pretence or hiding. It definitely hints that there is more to this woman that many might appreciate.

The repetition of "She" makes the poem more personal and makes it clear she is seen as worthy. Her connection to her past is shown by her playing songs from her past. Here the repetition of the town, "Bendigo" and Eaglehawk" emphasise her affection for her past, and by implication, her unwilling presence in the house she inhabited with her family afterwards. The abrupt listing of her life's experiences as "She had / Eight children, little money, many griefs" is summative and such negative experiences are clearly at odds with what she deserved. The summation is definite in its high modality. The fact that this list shares a line and runs into the next in some way implies that she was not the person who had the power in the household.

Amy Caroline's desire for power is seen in the final lines of the poem. Here the granddaughter remembers what her grandmother really wanted in life; she would have liked a cart to drive around the roads in. This seems a bit eccentric but seems to suit her rural background as this is a log wagon. Notably it is a big, powerful cart. The appendage of "of her own" implies she wanted ownership of it – which is the power. This memory is endearing as it is personal but so too does it reflect the grandmother's lack of freedom and choice. This implies the unfairness of the life she had to live – away from the place she loved.

Links to Texts and Human Experiences

Obvious by his absence is a grandfather. The audience knows nothing about him. This emphasises the plight of the grandmother as she seems alone in her adversity. In turn this helps show her endurance and fortitude. There were eight children so we have to assume her husband was around for a significant period. Perhaps it is he who does not really appreciate the hidden depths and complexity of this woman. His absence certainly makes the poem clearly a celebration of the grandmother. Similarly no time is spent on the children. It is obvious she loves all and the poet does not want attention distracted from the poem's central character. In many ways it is this resolute attention that shows that Amy Caroline deserves far more than she ever received in life.

The grandmother is shown as a positive figure and may represent women more generally, especially from her era. The phrase "Whatever chanced" reveals that women's lives are formed from fate not choice. She definitely did not choose to leave the country. It is significant that she did not want to be driven around, but wanted to drive herself. Here the driving is a metaphor for life and the control she wished she had. While we cannot know what situations contributed to her harsh life, the inequity involved in women's lives underpins this poem. It is a poem which helps the audience appreciate the harsh experiences many women tolerated, and still do today in a patriarchal society.

Questions for 'Amy Caroline'

1. In your own words, explain what is happening in this poem on a plot level.

2. There are no stanza breaks in this poem. How does that suit a poem of its subject?

3. How does Dobson work to create the aural effect of the grandmother's voice? How does this make the poem more effective for the audience?

4. Explain how the enjambment (run on lines) helps bring the audience closer to this personal poem?

5. List some aspects of the grandmother's life which are not mentioned. Explain why Dobson has focused on the aspects she has chosen; what is the comment on women's experience?

6. Consider the repetition of "She" in the poem. Is it uncreative or boring – or does it have a desired effect on the audience?

7. What is the effect of stopping after sorry and then forcing a new line? Why does Dobson force the pause?

8. Explain why the poem ends with the words, *of her own*. It might be seen as a little awkward. What is the intended effect?

9. Identify the aspects of the poem that make it clearly Australian. To what extent does this affect its comment on the human experience generally? (ie. Is it too specific?)

10. Complete your Reading Journal sheet/sheets for this poem.

'CANBERRA MORNING'

Glossary

stealthily	Secretive, secret or furtive
chatterers	Purposeless or foolish talk, rapid talk. Jabbering
haversacks	Bag worn over shoulder with straps
Sartre	Jean-Paul Sartre was a French philosopher, playwright, novelist, political activist, biographer and literary critic. He was a leader in French philosophy and Marxism. He challenged cultural and social assumptions about the world. He thought conformity was destructive and that 'Hell is other people'. He refused the Nobel Prize and influenced many thinkers of the period. *File:Flickr_-_Government_Press_Office_Israel_(GPO) Jean_Paul_Sartre_and_Simone_De_Beauvoir_welcomed_by Avraham Shlonsky and Leah Goldberg at Lod airport (14 March 1967)*
Top Forty	Usually referred to in terms of popular songs. The Top Forty refers to the forty most popular songs purchased by people over the course of a week. Back in the time of the poem it was physical vinyl records but now it is calculated on digital sales.
damn	To say something is bad, unfit, invalid or illegal, failure, condemnation. Also known as a word that is used to express anger and also a swear word.
slantwise	To veer or angle away from something, influenced by a subjective viewpoint or bias or personal feelings.

Poem Analysis

This poem traces a morning in Canberra from the perspective of the persona. The speaker is a watcher of the world around. On one level it is a simple poem, speaking of the newly risen sun, a bus-stop of children going to school and the bus's driver. On a deeper level the poem explores the dawning realisation, much like a new day, of the persona. There is a developed awareness of the freedom she has as an older person. You might choose to see it as a comment on the process of aging and the value that the persona comes to associate with it.

The poem begins with a description of the morning sun early in the day. It is a new day and it might be seen to symbolise the persona is ready for a new awareness. It may well be suggesting that time is like a hunter, The sun sends "long shadows". These are likened to a "stealthy" hunter like a cat as it hides "under parked cars". The metaphor is extended and the sun and hunter are paralleled. It is an image of potential energy; there is a latent energy of imminent action. There is a succession of long vowels such as those in "low", "creep", "parked" to create a quiet expectant atmosphere. It is a new day so it is an image of time and process, ready to spring on the unaware prey.

The prey is seen at the bus-stop. The bird image of the "flock of starlings" has energy and the excitement yet also ignorance of how it is being stalked. It is reminiscent of the flocks of wading birds at the waterhole watched by powerful predators. Here the poet is depicting the school children as a clear contrast to the quiet hunter. It is a sensual image that appeals to the audience – they are "chatterers" with "swinging haversacks" full of action, "pulling ribbons". With their youthful energy they are oblivious to any threats upon their way of life. They are unaware of time's effect on their lives but it is significant it lies in wait. Time has the power despite their ebullience. As they grow older the forces of society will bear on them. It will hunt them and their desires and perhaps turn them into people like their driver.

The third stanza speaks of the driver. Notably the description is not what he is doing but what he has in his pocket. The exotic sounding "Sartre" speaks of the philosophical work of Jean-Paul Charles Aymard Sartre. This is a clear mismatch with the dull, unskilled job he is doing. It is important that Sartre was renowned for his rejection of conformity and the limiting expectations of upbringing. This image symbolises the yearnings the driver has hidden and not able to be accessed in his job. It implies untapped potential and discontent. He is a grown up and lives a life following rules and expectations. This restriction is further supported by his moodiness. Indeed, he wears "dark glasses" which suggests he is hiding. Listening to the Top Forty may be an attempt to regain his youth which is being taken by time and seems squandered by this job. Perhaps you see the Top Forty as symbolic of the success he does not have or even the superficial existence he is caught up in. Either way time hunts him too, surrounding his bus.

The final stanza is a powerful statement in a certain tone: "life gets better as I grow older" The poem has moved from others to the persona. The personal move is indicated by the clear first person and the use of the colloquial language, "not giving a damn". Here the expletive gives force to the announcement. It seems a celebration of both the persona's knowledge and freedom. She is not hunted and is the one "looking slantwise". She is in control and sees "everyone's morning". Here "slantwise" suggests looking with a different perception. It is a seeing with wisdom and true perception. The highly modal "everyone" exaggerates her sublime understanding.

Links to Texts and Human Experiences

The poem is a set of observations by the watching persona. It is given weight by being set in the nation's capital. It is a poem with a lesson about the human experience. The statements are definite and the high modality of reinforces the omniscient persona who seems to know all. This adds authority to the observations and power to her realisation in the final stanza. Perhaps you see the poem as an acknowledgement of the power of the elderly. They can revel in understanding as they are free from social constraints and expectations. This is the link back to Sartre's work and the lesson that he hoped people could learn. Clearly his reader cannot act and Dobson may well be suggesting that it is time which will ultimately free us from the social constraints and expectations that hunt us.

Questions for 'Canberra Morning'

1. In your own words, explain what is happening in this poem on a plot level.

2. It is essential you read this poem correctly, following the punctuation. Practice reading it aloud. Do not rush it.

3. Explain how the image of the shadows as cats encourages the audience to see morning.

4. Explain how the enjambment (run on lines) helps contribute to the effect of the poem. Think what it does to the rhythm.

5. Analyse how stanza two uses language to create an energetic image of the children.

6. Analyse how stanza three uses language to create a staid image of the driver.

7. What is the comment about human experience given in the final stanza?

8. The poem begins as a distanced observation which then changes to a more personal comment in the final stanza. How does this add power to the final comment?

9. Describe the tone of the poem. Explain how it contributes to the effect of the poem.

10. Complete your Reading Journal sheet/sheets for this poem.

THE ESSAY

The essay consists of the basic form of an introduction, body paragraphs and conclusion. The esssay has been the subject of numerous texts and you should have the basic form well in hand. As teachers, the point we would emphasise would be to link the paragraphs both to each other and back to your argument (which should directly respond to the question). Of course, ensure your argument is logical and sustained.

Make sure you use specific examples and that your quotes are accurate. To ensure that you respond to the question, make sure you plan carefully and are sure what relevant point each paragraph is making. It is solid technique to actually 'tie up' each point by explicitly coming back to the question.

When composing an essay the basic conventions of the form are:

- State your argument, outline the points to be addressed and perhaps have a brief definition.

A solid structure for each paragraph is:
- Topic sentence (*the main idea and its link to the previous paragraph/ argument*)
- Explanation/ discussion of the point including links between texts if applicable.
- Detailed evidence (*Close textual reference – quotes, incidents and technique discussion.*)
- Tie up by restating the point's relevance to argument/ question

- Summary of points
- Final sentence that restates your argument

As well as this basic structure, you will need to focus on:

Audience – for the essay the audience must be considered formal unless specifically stated otherwise. Therefore, your language must reflect the audience. This gives you the opportunity to use the jargon and vocabulary that you have learnt in English. For the audience ensure your introduction is clear and has impact. Avoid slang or colloquial language including contractions (like 'doesn't', 'e.g.', 'etc.').

Purpose – the purpose of the essay is to answer the question given. The examiner evaluates how well you can make an argument and understand the module's issues and its text(s). An essay is solidly structured so its composer can analyse ideas. This is where you earn marks. It does not retell the story or state the obvious.

Communication – Take a few minutes to plan the essay. If you rush into your answer it is almost certain you will not make the most of the brief 40 minutes to show all you know about the question. More likely you will include irrelevant details that do not gain you marks but waste your precious time. Remember an essay is formal so **do not** do the following: story-tell, list and number points, misquote, use slang or colloquial language, be vague, use non-sentences or fail to address the question.

PLAN:

Don't even think about starting without one!

Introduce... the texts you are using in the response *Argument*: The human experience is affected by: ■ Idea One ■ Idea Two ■ Idea Three	You need to let the marker know what texts you are discussing. You can start with a definition but it can come in the first paragraph of the body. You MUST state your argument in response to the question and the points you will cover as part of it. Wait until the end of the response to give it!

↓

Idea One – Aspect of human experience as outlined in the textual material, e.g. physical impact. **Idea Two –** Another aspect of human experience as outlined in the textual material, e.g. psychological impact. ■ explain the idea ■ where and how is it shown in the prescribed text? ■ where and how is it shown in related text 1? **Idea Three** – People's sense of experience is affected by context and environment ■ explain the idea ■ where and how shown in the prescribed text? ■ where and how shown in related text 1?	You can use the things you have learned to organise the essay. For each one, you say where you saw this in your prescribed text and where in related text(s). Two or three ideas are usually enough as you can explore them in detail.

↓

■ Summary of two key ideas ■ Final sentence that restates your argument	Make sure your conclusion restates your argument. It does not have to be too long.

MODEL ESSAY OUTLINE

> **To what extent are human experiences significant in the set text?**
>
> **From your studies respond to this question using your set text and at ONE piece of other textual material**

This essay needs to be attacked in a manner that responds to the question and shows ALL your knowledge about the text. The question lends itself to a close study of the poetry of Rosemary Dobson as they show how the human experience is integral to life and how it shapes our other experiences and interaction with the world.

An introduction might be written:

> Human experiences are important in Dobson's poetry and the two related texts Lawrence's film *Jindabyne* and Ed Sheeran's song *Castle on the Hill*. These texts show how human experiences are integral to human existence and bring more meaning to one's life. Life is about experiences that challenge us and define how we see the world. They shape our beliefs and attitudes and can be confronting at the same time. Without experiences our lives would be empty and meaningless.

Your essay should then follow the outlined plan and develop these ideas. This gives you the opportunity to link the texts and fully develop each of the ideas.

ANNOTATED RELATED MATERIAL: DIFFERENT STUDIES OF HUMAN EXPERIENCES

Jindabyne – Ray Lawrence

Jindabyne is an Australian film that captures a wide array of human experiences. It touches on the ideas mentioned in the introduction to this text in a number of detailed instances. We can begin by considering the following before beginning a detailed examination of the narrative.

The collective human experience:

- Aboriginality and the spiritual;
- The Fishermen and their code;
- The reaction of the townsfolk;
- Media response;
- Interaction with the natural world.

Individual Experience:

- An individual character's response to the body – choose one;
- The killer;
- Response to the revelations;
- Past experiences and how they impact on current experiences;
- Reaction to loss – emotional;
- Assumptions about life.

We can now look at the plot to help us understand each of these issues. *Jindabyne* begins with the sound of a radio being tuned and the Australian feel of the movie is immediate with the theme music for the ABC news. Lawrence emphasises the isolation by having the radio not tune in correctly for an unknown female character, forcing her to use the cassette player. With this unusual beginning we know that her experience is not going to be positive.

We then pan to the rocks slowly where Gregory, our killer, sits patiently in a truck with the engine running watching the road. We know he is prepared for this as he has binoculars. He sees an Aboriginal girl, Susan O'Connor, driving and she is the one fiddling with the radio. He chases her down and forces her to stop. He moves toward her as we see a long shot of how isolated they are. We see his face in her window looming above her and screaming about the electricity coming down from the mountains. This film is no murder mystery, as we know from the beginning that the murderer is Gregory the electrician. This is about the experiences of the other characters in the film and how they respond to current experiences.

The Kane family, Stewart, Claire and son Tom, is waking. Claire pretends to sleep, before waking suddenly and being affectionate with Tom. Stewart and Tom head out fishing. The scene doesn't feel quite right and there is some emotional tension between Stewart and Claire that is unspoken due to what they have experienced in the past. Claire had a complicated past when she was pregnant with Tom. When she finds she is pregnant again, she becomes emotional and slightly unstable.

As the film builds we see the complex pasts of the characters and their interactions in the confinement of the small town. The fishing trip is a break from this and extremely important in their lives.

We see some of the emotional instability in characters such as Caylin-Calandria, who with Tom, has some issues at school. Along with Caylin-Calandria, Claire and Jude also have issues but in a nicely framed shot of the three female characters, we see them conform as members of a close knit group. The sacrifice they make is similar to Gregory's but on a different scale. Note the connection here and how each one is to get back to order and societal norms. This is the collective experience for all the characters.

At the Kanes' home the tensions are obvious from their past experiences but they contain it for appearances' sake. Occasionally, the tension reaches breaking point and the experience strains the superficial approach. The tension builds at home and the fishing trip seems like a good opportunity to break the cycle.

When we see Gregory dump Susan O'Connor's body in the river, we know that the fishing and her death will interact.

The next morning, the fishermen head off for their one big trip of the year and the sign 'Gone fishing' is put in the garage window. We see Billy on the phone to Elissa and putting the sign the wrong way round in the window shows his immaturity. They have already said they are taking him away to make a man of him. The four men have a few beers on the way and talk as they travel through the landscape. They intend to give Billy the experience they think he needs as a 'man' — a cultural rite of passage.

The men arrive and the high-tension electricity wires punctuate the wilderness. They begin to hike toward the valley. It's a long walk in and the terrain is hilly and difficult. They stop on the way and again we see Billy's naivety when Stewart says 'Listen to that' meaning the silence but he can't, as he has his earphones in. It is part of the break in tension of the film that they commune with nature. This experiential break affects all the men. The episode represents a distinct human experience.

Stewart wanders down the river fishing and sees Susan's body caught in the rocks. Hesitantly, he wades out to it and turns it over saying 'Oh Jesus' repeatedly. He screams for the others to come as he drags the body to the bank. He is obviously upset, making the sign of the cross. Stewart tells Rocco to 'take her, for fuck's sake, take her' and their shock is obvious. They all stare at the body and Billy goes to run off but they stop him. The four men meet and decide to leave her in the water and tie her so she doesn't float away.

The presence of the body threatens to detract from the enjoyment of the fishing experience. The act of attempted isolation of the bad experience is expected to evoke only a mild response. They do not anticipate the stormy reaction it receives when they return to the community.

The men go on fishing, with Stewart getting the first big fish on an absolutely perfect day. The lure of the fish is strong, especially when they see the big one he has caught. They have a successful and enjoyable time, a positive experience. They get a photo of the catch and Billy holds up his fish in a typical hunter/gatherer pose. Capturing an experience this way is most enjoyable.

It is a photo that will come back to haunt them as things change back in the world. An unanticipated adverse reaction can be a horrific experience.

Stewart goes to check on the dead girl, rolling her over and getting debris off her face in a quite tender gesture. The next day they head back and report it. At the car Billy rings Elissa and says they found a body but 'caught the most amazing fish'. They are told by the police to wait and seem despondent their trip has been ruined. They organise their story as Stewart says they have 'to get their story straight'.

We cut to Gregory eating breakfast and he appears to be a normal, lonely man until he goes out to his shed where he has hidden Susan's car and this reminds us of the evil in him. Consider his experience and his motivations. How does he see his actions and the world?

The next day at the station the policeman tells the fishermen 'we don't step over bodies for our recreational pursuits' and 'the whole town's ashamed of you'. When they are told to 'piss off' from the station the press are waiting for them and Billy makes a comment. Carl is angry with the press but we can begin to see signs of distress within the whole group.

The experience they had so looked forward to has become a negative one and the tensions we saw before are exacerbated by the emotional and collective response to the murder. Claire soon becomes obsessed with the whole affair because of her own state. The newspaper the next day has the headline, 'Men fish over dead body' because Billy has talked. Billy is late to work and Stewart tells him they have to 'stick together on this'.

Susan's sister calls them 'animals' and raises the race question by asking if they would have left a white girl. The Aboriginal youths begin to attack and vandalise the property of the men in violent

© Five Senses Education Pty Ltd

outbursts, including throwing a rock through Billy's van window and thus endangering his baby. They insult Carl at the caravan park and vandalise the garage.

The police aren't any help and the situation deteriorates. Jude tells the police they shouldn't be enforcing the 'political correctness' laws. The intervention of the sense of Aboriginality and race challenges the assumptions people have and how we see the world. The contrasting views are ingrained in the social structures and part of different collective experiences.

The Aboriginal people see the white people as 'interfering' and the group of fishermen begin to fight amongst themselves. Elissa says they shouldn't go to the bush at all as it's sacred. The group talk about the bush and Rocco punches Stewart for saying the Aborigines are superstitious. The experience of racial tension becomes ever-present and adds to the emotional responses to the experience.

We now head slowly to a resolution of the conflict brought about by the various experiences. Each is handled in a different manner by characters and you can explore one or two of the responses. To cycle back to the original murder, Claire is stalked by Gregory in his truck. He stops her but drives off after staring weirdly, an odd experience in itself.

Terry and Stewart talk and Stewart meets Rocco and Carl. He tells them Claire's left him 'again'. Rocco can't believe it and we cross cut to her looking out into the wilderness after he looks thoughtfully out the window. These different reactions to experiences mirror attitudes in life and reactions to emotional and intellectual conflict.

In conclusion, Lawrence takes us back to the healing power of nature in our human experiences when the Aboriginal people are having a ceremony. Gregory watches while Claire walks in. Again we see his truck as an omnipresent force in the film, almost an extension of him. An Aboriginal man tells Claire to 'piss off' from the ceremony after she says she has come to pay her 'respects' but he is told to leave her alone by an Auntie.

The smoke and tribal music symbolise the ceremonial nature of the setting and the camera pans around the scene and the bush. We see parts of the ceremony with chanting and clapping sticks. The camera moves in and out while other shots pan around the bush, giving us the full experience and Lawrence portrays this as a positive, healing experience.

Eventually Stewart, Tom, Carl, Jude and Rocco arrive to pay respects. Tom runs to his mother and Stewart goes over and says 'Sorry' but is rebuffed by the father who throws dirt on him and spits, refusing his apology. Then an Aboriginal girl tells a little about Susan's story and sings the last love song Susan wrote.

The camera pans around all the faces as they listen to the song and the ceremonial smoke wafts around. It seems to have some healing effect on everyone, as it is a meaningful experience which raises the idea of the spiritual experience in the text. The girl stops singing through emotion. 'Be gone' seems to symbolise in language the whole scenario for each character.

We see a long wide shot of the bush before fading back to Gregory waiting again in his car behind the rocks for another victim. It is quite a circular conclusion and it is an odd end when he crushes the fly. We don't quite know what to make of the whole experience and he seems to be the only character unchanged by the experiences in the film.

Poem: 'Inland' by John Kinsella

The poem captures the mood and ethos of the outback farming communities and deals with the human aspect more than some of the other poems in Kinsella's collection: *Peripheral Light*. This poem is one long restless thought that mimics memories and recollection while raising the current, topical issues that concern the poet. As usual with his poems Kinsella orientates the audience early with the word 'Inland' and then continues the poem without a full stop. The poem flows with the use of commas but Kinsella allows us to stop and think with the use of the colon, brackets and the hyphen. Look for these punctuation stops as you read as they emphasise a specific point or idea that resonates with the audience.

The first stanza gives us a foreshadowing of the events to follow with the warnings in the words 'storm', 'alert' and 'uncertain'. This ominous tone is reinforced by the word 'ghosts' and the implication of death which is constant in much of Kinsella's poetry. The next stanza deals with a more human element and we get the country feel with the bracketed gossip about McHenry's accident which shows the close knit community. Habits here are formed as part of survival and known to all as we see 'the old man plying the same track' and the families possibly heading to church on the Sunday morning.

The third stanza returns to the vagaries of nature. Kinsella repeats 'uncertain' with regard to the weather. Weather and the environment play a large role in farming communities and it is especially so at sowing and harvest. Despite the uncertainty and 'ashen' days which alter 'moods', the community returns to their habits and routines which shape their lives. The next stage returns to the road and the implication of a journey but a journey that is straight and in conflict with the cycles of the natural world. The path seems already marked and measured. It is 'straight and narrow', marked by a theodolite.

The final four lines of the poem are pure Kinsella, marking the transience of humanity on the landscape. We read

'it's a place of borrowed dreams
where the marks of the spirit
have been erased by dust –
the restless topsoil'

The European farmers had 'borrowed dreams' for their own relationship with the land but this line also harks back to the indigenous Dreamtime when the land was created. The indigenous view that the land owns the people is also true for Kinsella. This sense of nobody owning the land is strong in his poetry. European impact on the land can be seen in the spirituality being removed by the dust—dust created by the poor farming techniques transferred from a different land. He finishes with the 'restless topsoil' as if the whole earth is moving in its own discontented journey, just as the people move.

The influence here of genuinely lost spirituality and connection with the land as we move directly on the 'high road' contrasts with the more flowing, 'restless' side of the natural world. This visual contrast is obvious but we can also discuss the contrast between habit and spirit. 'Inland' is a poem that uses the landscape to show the contrast between two views of the countryside.

DRAMA: Eugene O'Neil's *Desire Under the Elms*

O'Neill sets out to instruct how the house and elms should appear and the year is 1850. Note how he describes the 'enormous' elms as,

> 'exhausted women resting their sagging breasts and hands and hair on its roof, and when it rains their tears trickle down monotonously and rot on the shingles'

and how they dominate and 'rot'. It is important to read this both in terms of the play and in the context of American theatre. The description here shows O'Neill's genius at new design and original theatricality.

Part One: Scene One

The whole first page and a third are nearly all playwright notes that describe the farm, the house and the characters of Eben, Simeon and Peter. The first words of the play, 'God! Purty!' reflect the beauty of the land and how Eben perceives it. Eben is 'resentful and defensive' and feels 'trapped' on the farm.

His older half-brothers Simeon and Peter are 'more bounce and homelier in face, shrewder and more practical.' They all have worked hard on their father's farm over the years and have little feeling for their absent father. We learn that Simeon had a 'woman' who died and that Peter is excited by the prospect of 'gold in the West'. They all talk about how hard they've worked and hope that the father might 'die soon'. What we get from all this is that they are earthy and this is reflected in their bodies and clothes which are all dirt stained.

We also see here the difference between them as Eben sees gold in the pasture, not California, as they head in for a dinner of bacon in what seems a ritual they have performed many times before. Note that O'Neill calls for the use of the curtain at the end of the scene.

Scene Two

It is twilight and again we get detailed notes on the interior scene. Simeon tells Eben he should not wish their father dead and Eben replies he's not his son but, 'I'm Maw – every drop of blood!' He then blames the father, Ephraim Cabot, for killing his mother by working her to death but the others just say there was work to be done. O'Neill gets them to list the jobs and Eben comes back with 'vengeful passion' that, while they did nothing, he will see his mother gets 'rest and sleep in her grave!'

They then discuss Cabot's absence and how he just drove off in a buggy one day in a rush. Simeon says that when he went,

> 'He druv off in the buggy, all spick an' span, with the mare all breshed an' shiny, druv off clackin' his tongue an' wavin' his whip. I remember it quite well'

Eben mocks Simeon for not stopping him and the scene concludes with Eben leaving to see Minnie the town whore. We learn all the Cabot men have slept with her. Simeon and Peter say that Eben is just like 'Paw' and thinks of California. The final image is of Eben with his arms stretched to the sky talking about starts and sin, 'my sin's as purty as any one on 'em!', until he 'strides' to the village for Min.

Scene Three

It is 'pitch darkness' and Eben comes home with the news that Cabot has married a 'purty' thirty-five year old. He has heard this in the village and this effectively disinherits the boys. Simeon and Peter see California as their only option now. Eben tells the boys that they can have three hundred dollars each if they sign their share of the farm over to him. He can get the money as his mother told him,

> 'I know whar it's hid. I been waitin' – Maw told me. She knew whar it lay fur years, but she was waitin'....It's her'n – the money he hoarded from her farm an' hid from Maw. It's my money by rights now.'

They think about it and Eben tells them about his night with Min. He tells how he hates the new wife after the boys suggest he might sleep with her, just like Min, to get the old man back. Peter and Simeon say they'll do the deal and leave the farm. Both are bitter and vindictive about Cabot.

Scene Four

The setting is the same as Scene Two and the boys are discussing how they don't have to work now – it is all down to Eben who is jubilant as he thinks it will all be his. Peter and Simeon again reflect on how like his father he is, 'Like his Paw'. They also tell he isn't much of a milker but they soon talk about their leaving and how they'll miss some aspects of the farm.

Eben comes back in and says that the 'old mule an the bride' are coming. The two older boys begin to pack and sign Eben's papers as he gives them the money Cabot had hidden. They tell him they'll send him 'a lump o' gold for Christmas' and head into the yard feeling 'light' because of their newfound freedom.

Ephraim Cabot and Abbie Putnam then come in and O'Neill describes them in detail. Cabot is

> 'seventy-five, tall and gaunt, with great, wiry, concentrated power, but stoop shouldered by toil. His face is hard as if it were hewn from a boulder, yet there is a weakness in it'

but his face is weakened with petty pride. Abbie is

> 'thirty-five, buxom, full of vitality. Her round face is pretty but marred by its rather gross sensuality. There is strength and obstinacy in her jaw, a hard determination in her eyes, and about her whole personality.'

She also has a 'desperate quality'. Cabot shows Abbie the place and she says to him it's 'mine'. Then he sees the two boys not working. He introduces Abbie and she goes to look at 'her' house and they warn her Eben's inside.

Cabot tells them to get to work and they give him cheek, saying they are 'free' and heading to California. They 'whoop' it up and he says he'll have them chained up. They throw rocks at the house, smashing the window and head off singing. Abbie sticks her head out the window and says she likes the room but he is thinking of the stock and 'almost runs' to the barn.

Abbie then meets Eben in the kitchen and talks to him in 'seductive tones'. She says she doesn't want to be his 'Maw' but friends and he cusses her. She tells him of her troubled life and how Cabot gave her a chance to escape it. He calls her a 'harlot' and they argue over ownership of the farm. She has the upper hand in law and he leaves but the seeds of their growing attraction have been set.

Outside he and his father argue about life and work and he tells Eben 'Ye'll never be more'n half a man!' The scene ends with Abbie washing up and the faint notes of the song the boys were singing as they left.

Part Two: Scene One

Again O'Neill describes in detail the farmhouse setting. Two months have passed and it is a hot Sunday afternoon. Abbie in her best outfit is sitting on the porch and Eben comes out of the house also dressed in his best. They stalk each other, both attracted and repelled. As he walks away she 'gives a sneering, taunting chuckle' at him and they argue but the attraction is obvious. She says that nature will pull him to her but he says that she is married and he goes to leave her.

She accuses him of going to Min and she gets angry stating he'll never get the farm,

> 'Ye'll never live t' see the day when even a stinkin' weed on
> it 'll belong t' ye!'

He says he hates her and leaves as Cabot enters. She tells him Eben has been mocking him and twists the conversation to the inheritance of the farm. She tells him Eben lusts after her and as he angers she backs off in her accusations. Reassured, he says that she can have the farm if she bears the son she says she wants with him. He says that he'd 'do anythin' ye axed, I tell ye!' if she gave him a son and tells her to pray to God for it to happen.

Scene Two

It is about eight in the evening and here the bedrooms are highlighted, with Eben in one and Cabot with Abbie in the other. The two of them are talking about a son. They seem together, yet apart, as he tells her of his life on the farm and how God's hard. He both lost and gained on the way through, but the farm is his. He says he is pleased he found her, his 'Rose o' Sharon'. Abbie promises him that she will bear a son as he basically threatens her,

> 'Ye don't know nothin' – nor never will. If ye don't hev a son t' redeem ye...'

and he leaves to sleep in the barn with the cows 'whar it's restful'.

We then see Eben and Abbie restless and she leaves the room and goes to him. He 'submits' to her kisses then 'hurls' her away. Abbie says she'd make him 'happy' and she knows he wants her too much. She tells him to go down to the parlour and he is shocked as this is where his mother was 'laid out'. She leaves for the parlour and he wonders what's happening. The scene closes with a question to his dead mother, 'Maw! Whar are yew?' but we know that he wants her and will go to her.

Scene Three

The scene now shifts to the parlour which is described as a 'grim, repressed room like a tomb'. Abbie waits and Eben appears and he sits at her invitation. They talk about his Maw and how they hate Cabot. Abbie throws herself at him with 'wild passion' and he is caught up in the moment and thinks that it's his Maw wanting him to sleep with Abbie to get revenge on Cabot,

I see it! I sees why. It's her vengeance on him – so's she kin rest quiet in her grave!

Abbie proclaims her love for him and he for her then they kiss 'in a fierce, bruising kiss' to close the scene.

Scene Four

A more bold and confident Eben leaves the house and Abbie opens the parlour window. She calls him over for a kiss and they talk a bit before Eben says his Maw can now rest. They split as Cabot comes out of the barn but are now obviously in love. Eben tells Cabot that his Maw is now at rest and Cabot says he rests best with the cows. Cabot is confused but the scene ends with him criticising Eben as 'Soft-headed' and a 'born fool' but, being a practical man, he heads for breakfast.

Part Three: Scene One

Time has passed to 'late spring the following year'. Eben is upstairs in emotional and psychological conflict while a party happens downstairs. Cabot has drunk too much and Abbie sits, pale and thin, in a rocking chair. There is a fiddler and Abbie begins the scene by asking for Eben and the guests 'titter' as most think the baby is Eben's, not Cabot's, which is true enough. They laugh and Cabot is angered by this and orders them to dance. The fiddler 'slyly' says they're waiting for Eben but Cabot mocks the boy and then ensues a bawdy conversation about his fertility,

> I got a lot in me – a hell of a lot – folks don't know on.
> Fiddle 'er up, durn ye! Give 'em somethin' t' dance t!'

The fiddler plays and they dance. Cabot joins in frantically and 'whoop(s)' it up. He exhausts the fiddler and pours whiskey. In the upstairs room Eben is looking at the baby. Abbie goes upstairs and Cabot leaves for outside, 'fresh air', as she has told him not to 'tech' her. The guests gossip after he goes and we see Eben and Abbie upstairs and she professes her love for him,

> 'Don't git feelin' low. I love ye, Eben. Kiss me.'

Cabot says he's going to rest in the barn. The scene concludes with the fiddler playing in celebration of 'the old skunk gittin' fooled!'

Scene Two

Eben is outside half an hour later and Cabot is coming back from the barn. Cabot tells him to get a woman inside and he might get a farm. Eben replies that this farm's his and Cabot mocks him. He tells her Abbie has been promised the farm for her son and Eben is angered thinking Abbie has tricked him.

Eben goes to kill her but Cabot is too strong for him and Abbie comes out to stop him choking Eben. Cabot tells him he's weak and goes inside to celebrate. Abbie tries to be tender with Eben but he rejects her and calls her a liar.

> 'Ye're nothin' but a stinkin' passel o' lies. Ye've been lyin' t' me every word ye spoke, day an' night, since we fust – done it. Ye've kept sayin' ye loved me....'

She says she loves him and tells him that the promise was made before they fell in love. He says he'll go to California.

They argue and he 'torturedly' says he wished the baby had never been born. Abbie is distraught and she says she'd kill the baby to prove her love for him. He says he won't listen to her but she calls after him that she can 'prove' she loves him and she 'kin do one thin' God does'. Abbie is desperate at the end of the scene.

Scene Three

It is now just before dawn and Eben is in the kitchen ready to leave. Abbie is near the cradle with 'her face full of terror'. She sobs but Cabot stirs and she goes to the kitchen and flings her arms around Eben, kissing him 'wildly'. She says 'I killed him' and he thinks she means Cabot but is horrified when she tells him it's the baby.

Eben states it was his baby and she says she loved it but loves him more. He is angered,

> 'Don't ye tech me! Ye're pizzen! How could ye – t' murder a pore little critter – Ye must've swapped yer soul t' hell!

and tells her that he is getting the Sheriff and heads, 'panting and sobbing' to town. She calls out to him that she loves him.

Scene Four

It is after dawn and Abbie is in the kitchen. Cabot wakes in his room and is concerned that he has woken late. He checks the baby and is proud it is quiet and asleep. He goes down to Abbie in the kitchen and she tells him the baby is dead. He runs to check and comes back down and asks 'why?'

In a rage she tells him it was Eben's son and that she loves Eben, not him. He blinks back a tear and then gets 'stony' so he can carry on and says he is going to get the Sheriff. Abbie tells him that Eben's already gone so that Cabot tells her he'll 'git t' wuk.' He then tells her he'd never have told and now he's going to be 'lonesomer'n ever!' Eben comes back and Cabot tells him to get off the farm.

Eben asks for her forgiveness and tells her he loves her. He says he realised he loved her at the Sheriff's and they have a chance to run away but Abbie says she'll take her punishment. Eben says he will share it with her and plans to tell the Sheriff they planned it together. They think they can stand it together and then Cabot comes back.

He goes into a long tirade and tells them how he's let the stock go and will burn the house down. He too plans to go to California but finds that Eben has gotten to his money first. Cabot says that this is a sign from God to him to stay and that 'God's hard an' lonesome!' At this point the Sheriff comes and Eben says he was involved with the baby's murder.

Cabot says 'Take 'em both' and leaves to get his stock. The sun is coming up and as they are led away Eben says the farm's 'Purty' and Abbie agrees. The Sheriff finishes the play with the line, 'It's a jim-dandy farm, no denyin'. Wish I owned it!'

OTHER RELATED TEXTS

Fiction / Non-fiction / Drama

- *Wonder* – R G Palacio
- *First they Killed My Father* – Luong Ung
- *The Graveyard Book* – Neil Gaiman
- *Looking for Alaska* – John Green
- *Eleanor and Park* by Rainbow Rowell
- *The Fault in Our Stars* – John Green
- *We All Fall Down* – Robert Cormier
- *The Old Man and the Sea* – Ernest Hemingway
- *The Fire Eaters* – David Almond
- *Ender's Game* – Orson Scott Card
- *Hatchet* – Gary Paulsen
- *Inside Black Australia* – Kevin Gilbert
- *Sapiens: A Brief History of Humankind* – Yuval Noah Harari
- *Peeling the Onion* – Wendy Orr
- *Raw* – Scott Monk
- *Six Degrees of Separation* – John Guare
- *The Book Thief* – Markus Zusak
- *When Dogs Cry* – Markus Zusak
- *Holes* – Louis Sachar
- *The Outsiders* – S.E. Hinton
- *Roll of Thunder, Hear My Cry* – Mildred D. Taylor
- *A Small Free Kiss in the Dark* – Glenda Millard
- *Monster* – Walter Dean Myers
- *Lord of the Flies* – William Golding
- *Jandamarra* – Steve Hawke
- *A Separate Peace* – John Knowles
- *A Monster Calls* – Patrick Ness
- *The Pigman* – Paul Zindel
- *The Invention of Hugo Cabret* – Brian Selznik

- *Emerald City* – David Williamson
- *Silent Spring* – Rachel Carson

Films and Television

- *The Human Experience* – Charles Kinnane
- *My Brilliant Career* – Gillian Armstrong
- *Broadchurch* – James Strong & Euros Lyn
- *Twinsters* – Samantha Futerman and Ryan Miyamoto
- *Be My Brother* – Genevieve Clay - Smith
- *What's Eating Gilbert Grape* – Lasse Hallstrom
- *Pleasantville* – Gary Ross
- *Eternal Sunshine of the Spotless Mind* – Michel Gondry
- *Taxi Driver* – Martin Scorsese
- *Tootsie* – Sydney Pollack
- *Back in Time for Dinner* – Kim Maddever
- *The Godfather* – Francis Ford Coppola
- *Friends* – David Crane and Marta Kaufmann
- *Dawson's Creek* – Kevin Williamson
- *Orange is the New Black* – Jenji Kohan
- *Boy Meets World* – Michael Jacobs and April Kelly

Website – quote on literature and the human experience

*http://view2.fdu.edu/academics/university-college/school-of-humanities/
english-language-and-literature-program/*

At its most fundamental level literature explores what it means to be a human being in this world and tries to describe what our human experience is like. As such, literature pushes us to confront the large human questions that have plagued humankind for centuries: issues of fate and free will, issues relating to our role in the universe, our relationship to God, and our relationships with others. Studying literature not only helps us to understand the complexity of these questions intellectually, but because of its very nature, it allows us to experience these tensions vicariously. Literature does not just tell us about human experience; it recreates it in a way we can feel and visualise. In other words, it calls for a total response from us—it stretches us beyond who we are.

First, literature can enhance our ability to relate to people. Because literature focuses on human relationships and self perception, it can broaden our own experience—to help us understand different kinds of people, different cultures, different problems—and, consequently, help us better understand our own relationships with others.

The study of literature also helps to foster an appreciation for beauty, symmetry, and order. This means more than the intuitive response of liking or disliking something we see or read or hear; it means a carefully thought-through response that will enhance appreciation—not destroy it.

Perhaps the most important skills that the study of literature teaches are analytic and synthetic skills. In learning to read carefully and analytically, we learn to ask hard questions both of the work and of ourselves. And as we seek to discover the relationships between the ideas and images we uncover in a work, our ultimate goal is to see the whole—to see how the parts work together to make the piece what it is. In grappling with the complex and difficult ideas contained in literature, we learn to accept the multiple dimensions and ambiguity that are so often present in life.

Finally, the study of literature will also help develop our writing abilities as we come to value the written word and understand its power to communicate.

Beyond all of these skills, however, it is not what literature can do for us as individuals as much as what it can do to us. Literature speaks to the whole person. Listen to it, says C. S. Lewis, and you will be changed.

Poetry

- 'Warren Pryor' – Alden Nowlan
- 'The Gardener' – Louis MacNeice
- 'The Improvers' – Colin Thiele

Songs

- *Be My Escape* – Relient K
- *Mandolin Wind* – Rod Stewart
- *Roxanne* – The Police
- *Wake Me Up When September Ends* – Green Day
- *Under Pressure* – Queen & David Bowie
- *Candle in the Wind* – Elton John
- *Empire State of Mind* – Alicia Keys
- *Gold Digger* – Kanye West
- *We Are Young* – Fun.
- *Centrefold* – J. Geils Band
- *It's Time* – Imagine Dragons
- *We Cry* – The Script
- *If I Were a Boy* – Beyoncé
- *Shake it Out* – Florence + the Machine
- *C'mon* – Panic! At the Disco & Fun.
- *I Don't Love You* – My Chemical Romance
- *Sing* – My Chemical Romance
- *1985* – Bowling for Soup
- *What About Me* – Shannon Noll
- *Sinner* – Jeremy Loops
- *7 Years* – Lucas Graham

- *Bitter Sweet Symphony* – The Verve
- *Ghost!* – Kid Kudi
- *Good Riddance (Time of Your Life)*   Green Day
- *Expectations* – Belle and Sebastian
- *After Hours* – We Are Scientists
- *Write About Love* – Belle and Sebastian
- *Trust Your Stomach* – Marching Band
- *Heaven Knows I'm Miserable Now* – The Smiths